TECHNOLOGY AND TEACHING

TECHNOLOGY AND TEACHING
Learning Skills

I. Muthuchamy
K. Thiyagu

KALPAZ

Published by

Kalpaz Publications
C-30, Satyawati Nagar,
Delhi – 110052
Ph.: 011-47034999, 9811692060
www.kalpazpublications.com
E-mail: kalpaz@hotmail.com

Distribution Network
gyanbooks.com
India, USA, Canada, UK, Australia, France

ISBN: 978-93-5722-727-8 (PB)

First Published, 2024

Printed at: Gyan Press, Delhi.

Technology and Teaching: Learning Skills
Author: I. Muthuchamy - K. Thiyagu

"India can become one of the developed countries in the world by 2020, if we adopt technology as our tool. For this, the teaching community should change its mindset and enthuse the students by means of technology."

Dr. A.P.J. Abdul Kalam,
Former President of India

Contents

Preface

In the field of Education, teaching is more effective being reaching the learners. Now, we are in the technological era and we are also marching towards millennium goals. Information and Communication Technologies (ICT's) have given birth to adopt newer techniques of teaching. This paradigm shift that brought about drastic changes in the objectives, contents and methods of teaching. The technological changes and developments, the process of teaching and learning also needs to change to face and meet the global opportunities and challenges. The ultimate aim is to improve the efficiency in teaching and learning by making use of technology in the classroom.

Here, a teacher should develop an adequate knowledge and skills for handling technology, besides, to equip minimum teaching skills and to know about different methods of teaching. Recognising the potentials of ICT and teaching cited above. It has been a pleasure to work on this book titled "Technology and Teaching-Learning Skills". We do hope that this book will be of immense help to students, teachers, researchers, professionals, educators and educational administrators.

This book is organised into five chapters. The first chapter attempts to present the computer application skills, highlighting the computer system and its functions and also highlighting the integration of ICT in teaching-learning and ICT applications. The second chapter devotes to communication skills, elements of communication, focussing the various types of communication, barriers of communication, methods of developing fluency in oral and written communication, class room communication and dynamics.

The third chapter explores the communication technology, computer mediated teaching like multimedia, e-content, satellite based communication and interpersonal communication through web. The fourth chapter discusses pedagogy, where instructional technology gives due importance, besides individualized instruction for small group instruction, large group instruction, teaching learning techniques like team teaching, group discussion, seminar, workshop, symposium and panel discussion. The last chapter gives the importance to teaching skills, focussing mainly on skill of set induction, skill of stimulus variation, skill of explanation, skill of probing questions, skill of black board work, skill of closure and evaluation of all those teaching skills.

The six chapter consists of the e-learning, types of e-learning, benefits, advantages and disadvantages of e-learning. The seventh chapter explores the components of mobile learning, types of mobile devices, mobile learning applications, advantages and disadvantages of mobile learning. The eighth chapter explains the definition of blended learning, dimensions of blended learning, benefits and criticism of blended learning. The ninth chapter explores the impor-tance of u-learning, combination of u-learning, benefits and criticism of u-learning.

I. MUTHUCHAMY
&
K. THIYAGU

1.

Computer Application Skills

COMPUTER SYSTEM

Computer system is a connection of electro-mechanical devices, that link together and forming a system in order to perform automatic electronic data processing (EDP) using software. It can manipulate and store data for the user when even it is required. It has the capacity to manipulate data to meaningful information. It is different from other processing machines such as punched cards, calculators etc, because it can also store instructions that will direct the machine to carry out the steps accordingly. Computer is an electronic device that computes or calculates numbers.

In other words, a computer is an electronic device with the ability to :

(*i*) Accept data supplied by the user.

(*ii*) Input, store and execute instructions.

(*iii*) Perform mathematical and logical operation.

(*iv*) Give results according to user's requirement

Definition of Computer

The following are the some of the definition of Computer

- "Computer is a fast operating electronic device which automatically accepts and store input data, processes them and produces results under the direction of a detailed step by step program".
- "Computer is an automatic electronic apparatus for making calculator or controlling operations that are expressible in numerical or logical terms".

- "The computer is an electronic device designed in such a way it automatically accepts and stores data input, process them and produce the desired output".
- "The computer is an electronic device, which converts raw data into valid and meaningful information".
- "The computer may be defined as an electronic device, which operates upon information data".

Diagram of Personal Computer

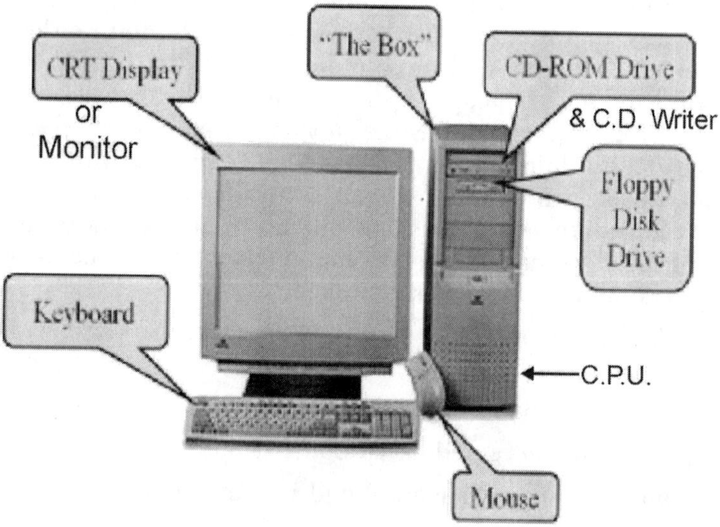

Characteristics of Computer

Now-a-days computer is playing a main role in everyday life it has become the need of people just like television, telephone or other electronic devices at home. It solves the human problems very quickly as well as accurately. The important characteristics of a computer are described below:

- *Celerity (High Speed)*: Computers are really very fast in their working. In a fraction of second, they can do millions of arithmetical operations. Because of this property, bus, railway and airline reservations are being very quickly with the help of computers. It denotes the speed of a computer. The computer present in the modern world has the speed of nano and pico second. The various speeds that are used by the computers from the former generations are as follows:

1 milli second = 1*10^-3 second

1 micro second = 1*10^-6 second

1 nano second = 1*10^-9 second

1 pico second = 1*10^-12 second

Thus the speeds are measured.

- *Accuracy*: In addition to speed, computers are also accurate in their output. If the data are feeded correctly to the computer, the output result will be accurate and free from errors. It denoted the accuracy of the computer. They are reliable and robust. It ever makes a mistake. Most probably the error occurs due to the user rather than the computer. There may be certain hardware mistake but with the advanced technique in hand they are overcome. Example: Only accurate robots are used to perform the operations for the patients since human hands are not flexible for making operations.
- *Storage capacity*: Computer has the facility to store large volume of data and other instructions and the data can also be retrieved whenever we need them. This storage capacity or computer memory is expressed in a unit called "Kilobyte", and 1Kb = 1024 bytes.
- *Repetitiveness*: A computer has the ability to perform a task given to it as many times as one desires. For example, if we wish to do arithmetic computation for ten million times, the computer will do that task without any hesitation. Moreover, even the last computation will be done with the same accuracy and speed as the first one.

- ***Versatility***: Versatile means flexible. Modern computer can perform different kind of tasks one by one of simultaneously. It is the most important feature of computer. At one moment you are playing game on computer, the next moment you are composing and sending e-mails etc. In colleges and universities computers are used to deliver lectures to the students. The talent of computer is dependent on the software.
- ***Automatism***: The computer will perform the required tasks until it meets the "stop" instruction in the programme, which means that once the computer has started the process of executing a programme, it will continue to work, until the programme is terminated. A computer can automatically perform operations without interfering the user during the operations. It controls automatically different devices attached with the computer. It executes automatically the programme instructions one by one
- ***Pertinacity (Endurance)***: This denotes that the computers never get tried as the humans do. If there are surplus amount of executions to be made then each and every execution will be executed at the same time period. They can perform their assigned task without taking any refreshment. Example: Computers which are used for controlling the satellites.
- ***Adaptabilty:*** In our day to day life computers has been a part, with their extended flexibility they are used, all over the world. They can be used as personal computers, for home uses, for business oriented tasks, weather forecasting, space explorations, institutions, railways, banking, medicine etc.
- ***Cheaper:*** Computers are short term investment in order to achieve a long term gain. Though the investment is high they reduce the cost of each and every transaction. They reduce man power and leads to an elegant and efficient way for computing various tasks.

- *Communications:* Today computer is mostly used to exchange messages or data through computer networks all over the world. For example the information can be received or send through the internet with the help of computer. It is most important feature of the modern information technology.
- *No Feelings:* Computer is an electronic machine. It has no feelings. It detects objects on the basis of instructions given to it. Based on our feelings, taste, knowledge and experience: we can make certain decisions and judgments in our daily life. On the other hand, computer cannot make such judgments on their own. Their judgments are totally based on instructions given to them.

Classification of Computers

- *Supercomputer:* The most powerful type of computer. These machines are special high-capacity computers used by very large organizations. For example, NASA uses supercomputers to track and control space explorations.
- *Mainframe computer:* It occupies specially wired, air-conditioned rooms. Although not nearly as powerful as supercomputers, mainframe computers are capable of great processing speeds and data storage. For example, insurance companies use mainframes to process information about millions of policyholders.
- *Mini computers:* It also known as mid range computers, are desk-sized machines. Medium-sized companies or departments of large companies typically use them for specific purposes. For example, production departments use minicomputers to monitor certain manufacturing process and assembly line operations.
- *Microcomputer:* The least powerful, yet are the most widely used and fastest-growing type of computer.

Categories of microcomputer include desktop, notebook, and personal digital assistants.

Different Generations of Computer

The history of computer development is often referred to in reference to the different generations of computing devices. Each generation of computer is characterized by a major technological development that fundamentally changed the way computers operate, resulting in increasingly smaller, cheaper, and more powerful and more efficient and reliable devices.

First Generation (1940-1956) Vacuum Tubes : First generation of computer was incorporated during the second world war by Germany to build a war plane while also in England was used to crack German secret codes and the mode of operation was the use of valves of about 1500 to 1800. The first computers used vacuum tubes for circuitry and magnetic drums for memory, and were often enormous, taking up entire rooms. They were very expensive to operate and in addition to using a great deal of electricity, generated a lot of heat, which was often the cause of malfunctions.

First generation computers relied on machine language, the lowest-level programming language understood by computers, to perform operations, and they could only solve one problem at a time. Input was based on punched cards and paper tape, and output was displayed on printouts. The UNIVAC and ENIAC computers are examples of first-generation computing devices.

Second Generation (1956-1963) Transistors: Second generation was made, and there was just a little change to the first generation and its mode of operation was the transistor instead of valves, these computers were used for calculation of great figures as well as scientific applications. Transistors replaced vacuum tubes and ushered in the second generation of computers. The transistor was invented in 1947 but did not see widespread use in computers until the late

1950s. The transistor was far superior to the vacuum tube, allowing computers to become smaller, faster, cheaper, more energy-efficient and more reliable than their first-generation predecessors. Though the transistor still generated a great deal of heat that subjected the computer to damage, it was a vast improvement over the vacuum tube. Second-generation computers still relied on punched cards for input and printouts for output.

Second-generation computers moved from cryptic binary machine language to symbolic, or assembly, languages, which allowed programmers to specify instructions in words. High-level programming languages were also being developed at this time, such as early versions of COBOL and FORTRAN. These were also the first computers that stored their instructions in their memory, which moved from a magnetic drum to magnetic core technology. The first computers of this generation were developed for the atomic energy industry.

Third Generation (1964-1971) Integrated Circuits: Third generation computer was designed to suite a small piece of space and its mode of operation was based on silicon and its used large silicon integrated circuit. The development of the integrated circuit was the hallmark of the third generation of computers. Transistors were miniaturized and placed on silicon chips, called semiconductors, which drastically increased the speed and efficiency of computers. Instead of punched cards and printouts, users interacted with third generation computers through keyboards and monitors and interfaced with an operating system, which allowed the device to run many different applications at one time with a central program that monitored the memory. Computers for the first time became accessible to a mass audience because they were smaller and cheaper than their predecessors.

Fourth Generation (1971-Present) Microprocessors : Forth generation computers was also designed to suite a small piece of space and its mode of operation was based on silicon of very large silicon integrated circuit (VLSI) and ultra large silicon integrated circuit (ULSI). The microprocessor brought the fourth generation of computers, as thousands of integrated circuits we rebuilt onto a single silicon chip. A silicon chip that contains a CPU. In the world of personal computers, the terms microprocessor and CPU are used interchangeably. At the heart of all personal computers and most workstations sits a microprocessor. Microprocessors also control the logic of almost all digital devices, from clock radios to fuel-injection systems for automobiles.

Three basic characteristics differentiate microprocessors:

- *Instruction Set:* The set of instructions that the microprocessor can execute.
- *Bandwidth:* The number of bits processed in a single instruction.
- *Clock Speed:* Given in megahertz (MHz), the clock speed determines how many instructions per second the processor can execute.

Fifth Generation (Present and Beyond) Artificial Intelligence: Fifth generation of computer is the development of softwares to enhance computer works and its robotic applications. Fifth generation computing devices, based on artificial intelligence, are still in development, though there are some applications, such as voice recognition, that are being used today. The use of parallel processing and superconductors is helping to make artificial intelligence a reality. Quantum computation and molecular and nanotechnology will radically change the face of computers in years to come. The goal of fifth-generation computing is to develop devices that respond to natural language input and are capable of learning and self-organization.

Fifth generation computing devices, based on artificial intelligence, are still in development, though there are some applications, such as voice recognition, that are being used today.

Artificial Intelligence is the branch of computer science concerned with making computers behave like humans. The term was coined in 1956 by John McCarthy at the Massachusetts Institute of Technology. Artificial intelligence includes:

- *Games Playing:* programming computers to play games such as chess and checkers.
- *Expert Systems:* programming computers to make decisions in real-life situations (for example, some expert systems help doctors diagnose diseases based on symptoms).
- *Natural Language:* programming computers to understand natural human languages.
- *Neural Networks:* Systems that simulate intelligence by attempting to reproduce the types of physical connections that occur in animal brains.
- *Robotics:* programming computers to see and hear and react to other sensory stimuli.

Five Basic Operations of Computer

The computer performs the five basic operations to carry out any task and they are Input, Process, Output, Storing and Controlling. Most of you might be knowing about these basic operations.

1. *Input:* It is the process of capturing or acquiring the information, or it is the process of accepting data or information, by using input the computer can do any process.
2. *Process:* It is the transformation process to convert the input into output.
3. *Output:* It is the result, which comes from the transformation process or it is the outcome of the process.
4. *Storing:* It is the process of storing or retaining the data or information or instructions, so that the user can retain and retrieve it whenever required.

5. ***Controlling:*** It is the process of directing the manner and sequence in which all the operations are to be performed.

COMPONENTS OF A COMPUTER/PARTS AND THEIR FUNCTION

Any computer has the following essential components.

They are

(*i*) Input Devices

(*ii*) Central Processing Unit (CPU)

  (*a*) Arithmetic and Logic Unit

  (*b*) Control Unit

  (*c*) Memory Unit and

  (*d*) Registers

(*iii*) Output Devices.

The following block diagram shows the fundamental components of a digital computer.

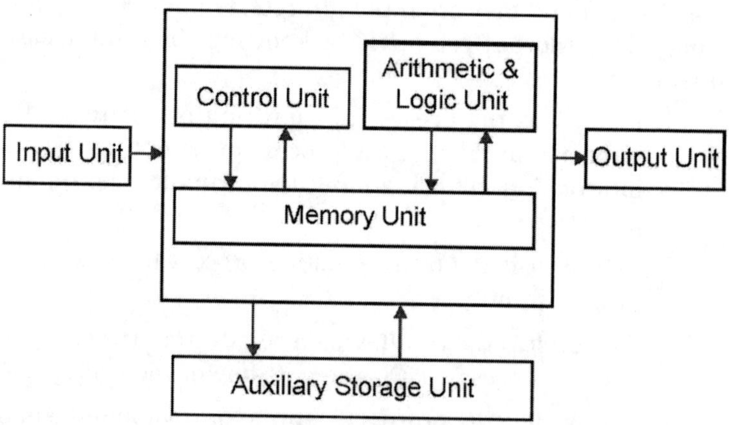

Fig. Block diagram of the Essential Components of a Computer

Essential Components of a Computer

(*i*) ***Input devices:*** They are the tools through which one can feed the data into the computer. In other words, an input device will be the medium through which one can communicate with the computer. There are so many input devices available for a computer. A mouse, keyboard, light pen, microphone etc., are the commonly used input devices in a digital computer.

(*ii*) ***Central Processing Unit (CPU):*** It is considered to be the heart of the computer system, which consists of (*a*) Arithmetic and Logic Unit, (*b*) Control Unit, (*c*) Memory unit and (*d*) Registers. The CPU executes the instructions as soon as the computer gets instructions from an input device.

(*a*) ***Arithmetic and Logic Unit (ALU):*** This unit performs a number of arithmetic operations such as, addition, subtraction etc. and also performs the logical opera-tions.

(*b*) ***Control Unit:*** The Control unit controls the entire operations of all the units of a computer. It brings one instruction at a time from the memory, interprets it and obeys it by coordinating the working of all the others units. In other words, this unit is considered to be the nervous system of a computer. All the commands are regulated and controlled by this unit.

(*c*) ***Memory Unit:*** This unit consists of locations or cells on which the data can be stored. If you want to retrieve the data, the data can be retrieved from the same unit. This unit consists of two types of memories viz., Permanent memory and secondary or auxiliary memory. A permanent memory is nothing but the semiconductor memory device available within the computer. Hard disk is an example of permanent memory device. The secondary memory is the memory which is movable and can be taken away from the computer and can be kept safely. Floppy disks, Compact discs and memory sticks are the examples of secondary memory devices.

(*d*) ***Registers:*** They are used to store data and information for future application and uses.

(*iii*) ***Output Devices:*** The output devices are the devices through which a computer gives the results, which can be in the form of graphs, or tables, or printed reports. The commonly available output units are (i) a monitor or TV screen, also called a Visual Display Unit (VDU), (ii) a printer (iii) a plotter and iv) speaker.

Input and Output Devices

Input Devices: Input devices are those devices through which the data can be fed into the computer. The most common input devices are listed below :

(a) Keyboard

(b) Mouse

(c) Light Pen

(d) Track Ball

(e) Track Pad

(f) Joy Stick

(g) Touch Screen

Alternate Input Devices

(h) Optical Mark Reading and Recognition (OMR)

(i) Optical Character Recognition (OCR)

(j) Magnetic Ink Character Recognition (MICR)

(k) Bar coding

(l) Scanner

(a) Flatbed Scanner

(b) Overhead Scanner

(c) Hand Held Scanner

(m) Speech Input Unit.

(n) Graphics Tablet.

(a) Key board: The most common way of entering data into a computer is through the keyboard. The layout of the letters on a keyboard is standardized across many countries in the world and is called a QWERTY keyboard. These are the first few characters on the top row of the letters. Each key acts as switch which closes when the key is pressed. The computer's processor scans the keyboard hundred of times per second to see if a key has been pressed. When a key is pressed, a code that depends on which key has been pressed is sent to the processing unit.

(b) Mouse: It is a very small handheld device through which one can control cursor movements in any direction. It has to be held in hand and may be pushed in a flat and smooth surface. There are several types of mouses that are available in the computer field. They are scroll mouse, optical mouse, and cordless mouse and so on. There are two separate click buttons available in a mouse through which one can perform the specific task or can reach a specific menu.

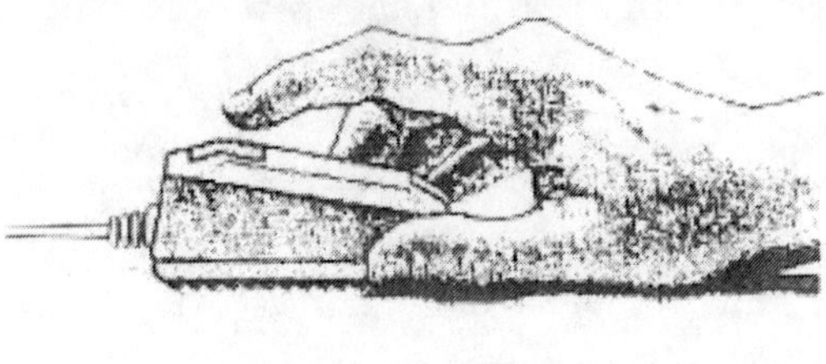

(c) Light Pen: The light pen is one of the first point devices. It looks like a ballpoint pen connected to the computer by a cable. This instrument can be used in conjunction with a video display. It has a photoelectric cell unit's tip that identifies its current location and sends this information via an electrical impulse to the computer. These pens are used frequently for drawing. The software traces the movement of the pen's light on the screen, filling in the lines you draw. You can then use the light pen to select items displayed on the screen by touching the pen to the items. However, as a selection device, the light pen is not as effective as the mouse.

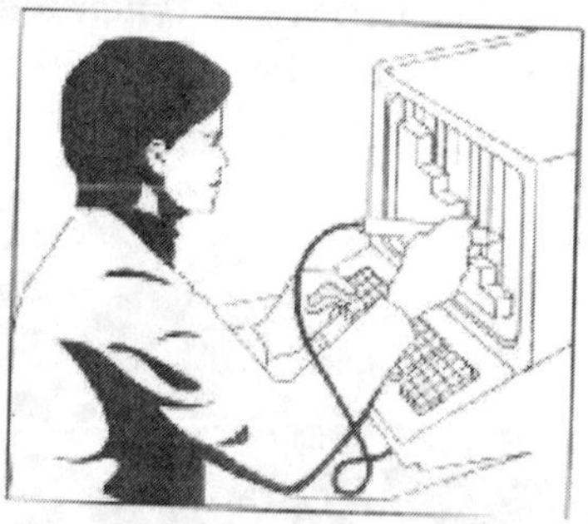

(d) Track Ball: The Track ball, which performs the same tasks as the mouse, operates with a rotating metal ball inset in a small, boxlike device and does not require a desktop. With your fingers, you can roll the exposed part of the trackball, producing cursor movement on the screen. This device was very popular in portable computers.

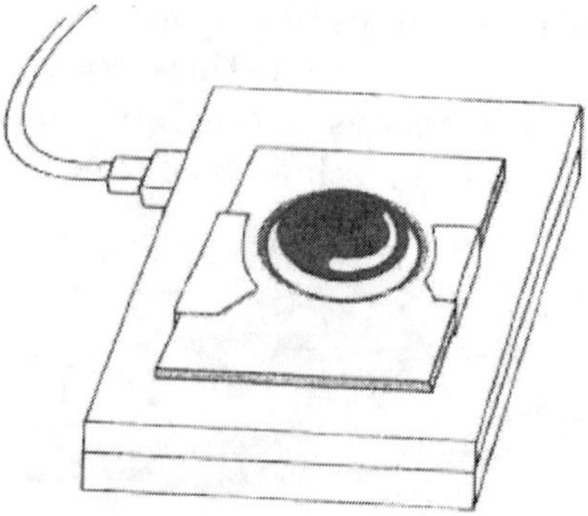

*(e) **Track Pad:*** The track pad is a pressure-sensitive pad that is smaller, more accurate, thinner, and less expensive to build than the trackball. It senses distortions in an electrical field caused by the positive charge of a fingertip. When you push your finger up on the pad, the cursor moves up on the screen. This device does not use absolute cursor positioning but relative cursor positioning, which means that a place on the pad's surface does not correspond to a relative location on the computer screen. The faster your fingers travel on the pad, the greater the distance you will cover on the computer screen.

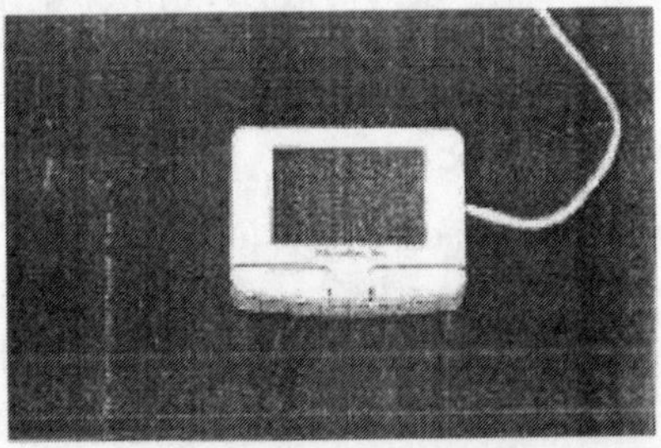

(f) Joy Stick: The joystick is a small box with a moving stick and buttons, is used primarily for games, educational software and CAD systems. You manipulate the stick to position the cursor and click on a button to send impulses to the computer. The joystick does not interfere with your view of the screen nor does it require the movement of an object (like a mouse). A joystick is fun to use, because of the speed with which it moves the cursor on the screen, but it is awkward in selecting items from a menu which is strength of the touch screen.

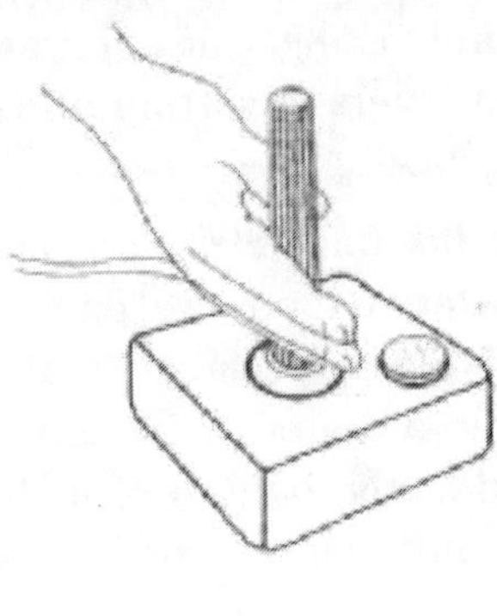

(g) Touch Screen: Touch screens are easy to use (user friendly) and might be found as input devices in public places (e.g. museums or building societies.) On touch-sensitive screens there are crisscrossing beams of infrared light just in front of the glass on the computer monitor. When a user touches the glass with the finger, two sets of rays are blocked: the rays traveling from side to side (y coordinates) and the rays going from top to bottom (x coordinates). The computer can detect the position of the finger from the light sensors placed on the opposite side of the monitor screen to the light sources, and respond accordingly.

Alternate Input Devices

(h) Optical Mark Reading and Recognitions (OMR): Optical mark readers detect marks made on paper. It is usually recommended that the marks are made with a soft (HB) pencil. The reader scans the paper with an infrared light. Where there is no mark, there is a strong reflection of light off the white paper; where a mark has been made, the reflection is reduced. School registers and some multiple-choice examination papers use this type of input device.

(i) Optical Character Recognition (OCR): Scanning devices using OCR software are used to recognize letters, numbers and words. The ability to scan the characters accurately depends on how clear the writing is. Scanners have been improved to be able to read different styles and sizes of text as well as neat handwriting. One application of OCR is reading the postcodes on letters at sorting offices so that letters can be sorted automatically.

(j) Magnetic Ink Character Recognition (MICR): In this technique, characters with are readable by us are printed on documents by using a special type of ink. This method of inputting data into a computer is used on bank cheques. The numbers printed at the bottom of a cheque have magnetic particles in the ink. These can be read very quickly by

machines. Three numbers are printed on a cheque: the cheque number; the bank or building society sort code; and the customer's account number. When a cheque is written and presented to the bank (paid in), a fourth number is added using special magnetic ink, which can be read by the computer. This last number to be typed on the cheque by the bank is the amount the cheque is made out for. MICR is very reliable as a means of entering data into a computer because it can read even if someone writes over the numbers with a pen.

(k) Bar Coding: This is also an important input device. In this, small strip like lines with varying thickness and spacing are printed on books, packages etc, which are read by optical readers and converted into electrical pulses. These patterns of lines are unique and standardized. Bar codes are made up of black and white stripes of different thickness. These lines represent numbers and are read with a wand or laser scanner.

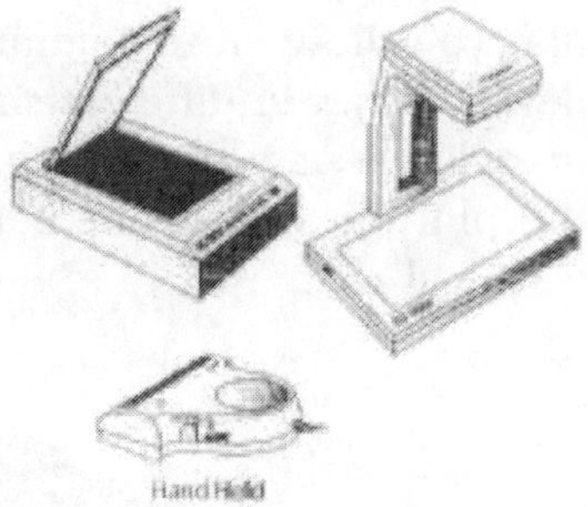

(l) Scanner: The scanner transforms images or printed text into electronic images or text. It is a digitize photographs or line art and store the images as a file that can be transferred into a paint program or directly into a word processor. If you create a newsletter and want to insert a picture into the text, you scan the picture, copy it, and then 'paste' it into the document. Scanners used for this purpose come in a variety of forms: (*a*) Flatbed Scanner, (*b*) Over Head Scanner and (*c*) Hand Held Scanner.

(a) ***Flatbed Scanner:*** It easily scans documents, books, or periodicals. You simply open the lid of the scanner and place the materials on the 'bed'.

(b) Over Head Scanner: The Overhead scanner scans large documents as a flatbed does. It also scans three-dimensional objects.

(c) Hand-Held Scanner: It fits in the palm of your hand. You slide it across the image or document slowly, at the rate of about an inch every ten seconds. It works well on four-inch columns, but it is not able to scan an entire line of text in a single pass. The only alternative is to stitch or paste the material together, which is time consuming but does produce acceptable results.

(m) Speech Input Unit: In this speech unit, spoken words have been taken by the unit as its input and converted into a form which can be understood by the computer. In Windows XP version, there is a provision for speech recognition known as narrator. One can give instructions to the computer by using a microphone attached to the CPU.

(n) Graphics Tablet: The graphics tablet is a plotting tablet that you draw on to communicate with the computer. This device comes in different sizes and is accompanied by pens or styluses. As you draw, making contact with the surface of the plotting board, the computer detects a difference of electrical charges.

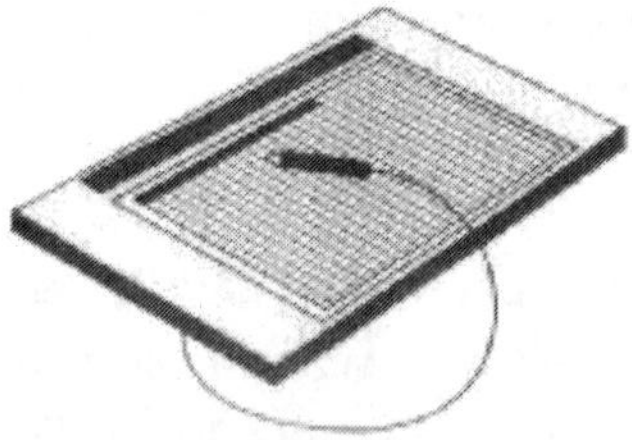

Output Devices

Output devices enable your computer to communicate with you. This enables you to see the results of a calculation, the text you have typed, and many other things. Without an output device, you will not be able to communicate with your computer and thus you will not be able to control or work on your computer. The two main output devices are monitors, and printers. The other output devices are plotters, image setters, and sound system and so on.

(a) Monitors: Monitors are the most commonly used output device of a computer. This can facilitate the user to visualize the result. It looks like a regular Television. They are of different types and they have different display capacities (otherwise known as adapter cards). The following are some commonly available adapter cards.

- Colour Graphic Adapter (CGA)
- Enhanced Graphic Adapter (EGA)
- Video Graphic Array (VGA)
- Super Video Graphics Arrays (SVGA)

A pixel is a frequently used term in a computer monitor. It is nothing but a smallest dot that can be displayed by the monitor. They are responsible for the resolution of a monitor, which determines the quality of a monitor. The data or the results displayed by the monitor are technically known as a soft copy.

Liquid crystal displays or LCD monitors are commonly found on laptop computers because they are more compact than CRT monitors. The liquid crystals are clear in their normal state, but they become opaque when charged with electricity. LCD monitors are also available in colour, but the clarity of the display is not as great as the CRT monitor.

(b) Printers: There are several types of printers available in the market. The printers are used to take a copy or number of copies of the result or the data. The printout from a printer is technically known as a hard copy. The printers can be classified as follows.

(*i*) Line printers

(*a*) Drum Printers

(*b*) Chain Printers

(*ii*) Serial printers or Dot matrix Printers

(*iii*) Inkjet printers or letter quality Printers

(*iv*) Laser printers.

(i) Line Printers: These printers will print a complete line at a time. The printing speed may vary from 90 to 160 characters on a 15-inch line. They print eight lines per vertical inch. Sixty four to ninety six character sets are usually used with English letters.

There are two types of line printers. They are:

(*a*) Drum Printers: These types of printers consist of a cylindrical drum and the characters to be printed are embossed on its surface.

(*b*) Chain Printers: In this printer, the character sets are embossed on a steel band.

(ii) Serial Printers or Dot Matrix Printers: Dot-matrix printers use a set of pins on a print head to create an image on a page. The print head moves back and forth across the age while the pins strike the paper in different combinations, through an inked ribbon. The quality of the image improves with a greater number of pins. Earlier dot-matrix printers had nine pins resulting in a vertical resolution of only nine dots. Newer models have 24 pins resulting in a greater overlap of dots and less white space, or higher resolution.

(iii) Ink Printers or Letter Quality Printers: Ink-jet printers spray ink from a set of small nozzles directly onto paper. Up to 64 nozzles are located on the print head which sweeps across the page line by line, much like a dot-matrix printer. The resolution of an ink-jet printer is higher than a dot-matrix printer, but its output is not as clear as that of a laser printer. Ink-jet printers are capable of bright, colour output.

(iv) Laser Printers: Laser printers use a separate small computer, as well as a laser and toner, to produce an image. The printer's computer interprets the data from the microcomputer and controls the laser. The laser charges a drum, which then picks up particles of ink having an opposite electronic charge, called toner. The toner is transferred from the drum to paper using heat and pressure, much like a photocopier. Unlike dot-matrix printers, laser printers are quiet and produce higher quality output. Resolution on a laser printer is measured in dots per inch or DPI. An average printer can have 300 DPI while a high-end laser printer can have 1800 DPI.

Secondary Memory or Auxiliary Memory

These types of memory are the additional memory devices used to store the data or programmes permanently. In other words, they are known as magnetic surface recording devices. Some commonly used secondary memory devices are given below:

(*i*) Hard disks

(*ii*) Floppy disks

(*iii*) CD ROMs

(*iv*) Digital Versatile Disks (DVD)

(*v*) Magnetic tapes and so on.

Hard Disks: Hard disks are a common form of data storage on most computers. It is used to store the operating system (e.g. Microsoft ® Windows), applications such as word processors, spreadsheets, databases, games and the data from programmes. Data are stored by magnetizing the surface of a flat, circular plate. These plates rotate at high speed (60 to 120 revs per seconds). A read/write head floats on a cushion of air a fraction of a millimeter above the surface of the disk. The drive is in a sealed unit to protect it. Hard drives usually consist of several disks on a single spindle. Each disk is able to store data and this has the advantage that each surface can have its own read/write head. A typical PC will have a hard disk capacity of between 40G Band 80 GG.

Floppy disks: Most computers come with a 3.5 – inch disc drive. The 3.5 inch discs are used to transfer small amounts of data between computers. Before data is stored on a disc, the disc needs to be formatted. This creates a magnetic map of the disc surface to enable the data to be either read from the disc or written onto the disc, very quickly.

CD ROMs (Drives): CD-ROM drives use the same technology as music CDs and CD players. The data is stored on the disk digitally and a laser beam is used to read the data off the disc. Because light is used to read the disc, the data may be packed closely and the disc therefore has a large capacity. Because of their huge storage capacities they are useful for distributing software, storing clip art and use in multimedia systems. CD-ROMS are read-only discs, which mean that you can read data off the disc but not alter it or store new data. A CD recordable (CD-R) drive has a read/ writes capability. Standard CD-R discs can be written to only once, but there is a type of disc called CD-RW that with a suitable drive can be written, erased and rewritten.

Digital Versatile Disks (DVD): Digital versatile discs are similar to CD-ROMS in that they look identical and are used to store lots of data. Like CD-ROMs, they are used to store computer application software, multimedia programmes (encyclopedias) and full-length movies. A DVD can replace six to seven CD-ROMS. A CD –ROM stores 700 MB of data, whereas a DVD typically stores 4.7 GB (4700 MB). DVD's are used to store movies and produce much better quality pictures and sound compared to normal videotape.

Magnetic tapes: Large spools of tape are used by very large computer systems that need to hold huge amounts of data. Their main use is for making backup (security) copies of hard discs. Data is stored along the tape in blocks, separated by 'interlocking gaps' Just like the tape in a tape-recorder, the data is written to or read from the tape as it passes the magnetic heads. One disadvantage of tape storage is that you cannot go directly to an item of data on the tape as you can with a disk. It is necessary to start at the beginning of the tape and search for the data as the tape goes past the heads- this is called serial access.

OPERATIONS OF COMPUTER

Switch off / shut down

1. Click the Start button. The Start menu will appear.
2. Click Turn Off Computer. The Turn Off Computer dialog box will appear.
3. Click the Turn Off icon. Your computer will shut down.

Restart

You may need to shut down and restart your computer after installing a new program or if your system becomes unstable. To shut down and immediately restart your computer:

1. Click the Start button. The Start menu will appear.
2. Click Turn Off Computer. The Turn Off Computer dialog box will appear.
3. Click the Restart icon. Your computer will restart.

Start a Programme

1. Click the Start button, located in the lower left corner of your screen.
2. Highlight Programs. The Programme menu will appear.
3. Move to the Programme menu and highlight the program you want to start. If you see a right pointer next to your selection, a submenu will appear. Refine your choice by highlighting the appropriate selection on the submenu. Continue until you get to the final submenu.
4. Click the program name to start the programme.

Standby Mode

When your computer is in the Standby mode, your computer consumes less electricity, but is ready for immediate use. However, if the computer loses electrical power while in the standby mode, any information you have not saved will be lost.

1. Click the Start button. The Start menu will appear.
2. Click Turn Off Computer. The Turn Off Computer dialog box will appear.
3. Click the Stand by icon.

Mouse Operations / Mouse Control

A device that controls the movement of the cursor or pointer on a display screen. A mouse is a small object you can roll along a hard, flat surface. Its name is derived from its shape, which looks a bit like a mouse, its connecting wire that one can imagine to be the mouse's tail, and the fact that one must make it scurry along a surface. As you move the mouse, the pointer on the display screen moves in the same direction. Mice contain at least one button and sometimes as many as three, which have different functions depending on what program is running. Some newer mice also include a ***scroll wheel*** for scrolling through long documents.

Invented by Douglas Engelbart of Stanford Research Center in 1963, and pioneered by Xerox in the 1970s, the mouse is one of the great breakthroughs in computer ergonomics because it frees the user to a large extent from using the keyboard. In particular, the mouse is important for graphical user interfaces because you can simply point to options and objects and click a mouse button. Such applications are often called ***point-and-click*** programs. The mouse is also useful for graphics programs that allow you to draw pictures by using the mouse like a pen, pencil, or paintbrush.

There are three basic types of mice:

1. ***Mechanical:*** Has a rubber or metal ball on its underside that can roll in all directions. Mechanical sensors within the mouse detect the direction the ball is rolling and move the screen pointer accordingly.
2. ***Optomechanical:*** Same as a mechanical mouse, but uses optical sensors to detect motion of the ball.

3. ***Optical:*** Uses a laser to detect the mouse's movement. You must move the mouse along a special mat with a grid so that the optical mechanism has a frame of reference. Optical mice have no mechanical moving parts. They respond more quickly and precisely than mechanical and Optomechanical mice, but they are also more expensive.

A mouse typically controls the motion of a cursor in two dimensions in a graphical user interface (GUI). Clicking or hovering (stopping movement while the cursor is within the bounds of an area) can select files, programmes or actions from a list of names, or (in graphical interfaces) through small images called "icons" and other elements. For example, a text file might be represented by a picture of a paper notebook, and clicking while the cursor hovers this icon might cause a text editing program to open the file in a window.

Different ways of operating the mouse cause specific things to happen in the GUI:

- Click: pressing and releasing a button.
  - (left) Single-click: clicking the main button.
  - (left) Double-click: clicking the button two times in quick succession counts as a different gesture than two separate single clicks.
  - (left) Triple-click: clicking the button three times in quick succession.
  - Right-click: clicking the secondary button.
  - Middle-click: clicking the ternary button.
- Drag: pressing and holding a button, then moving the mouse without releasing. (Use the command "drag with the right mouse button" instead of just "drag" when you instruct a user to drag an object while holding the right mouse button down instead of the more commonly used left mouse button.)

- Button chording (a.k.a. Rocker navigation).
  - Combination of right-click then left-click.
  - Combination of left-click then right-click or keyboard letter.
  - Combination of left or right-click and the mouse wheel.
- Clicking while holding down a modifier key.

Keyboard and Some Functions of Key

The computer keyboard is the basic device through which you input information into the system. Though many other forms of inputting devices have come out in the market today, there is nothing equivalent to the keyboard. Using the keyboard is easy because most of them have the QWERTY typewriter set up. There are other set-ups also available such as Dvorak, ABCDE, XPeRT, QWERTZ and AZERTY. Each of these set-ups offer different typing comfort and you based your choice on how quickly you can use them to type information.

There are many tasks that you can accomplish using the keyboard. You can use it to type out your documents, access menus, manipulate your system and much more. The keyboard also includes shortcut keys that enable you to carry out certain tasks more easily and quickly using just the keyboard. Usually a keyboard has something between 80 to 110 keys. The difference in the keys set up is based on many factors such as board's manufacture, the operating system they are made from, whether they are part of a PC system or they are part of a laptop or hand-held device.

In addition to the typing keys, the keyboard also has a numeric keypad through which you can input numbers. It has control keys like Home, Page Up, Page Down, Insert, Delete, End, Control (Ctrl), Alternate (Alt), and Escape (Esc) that let you carry out these simple tasks with just one click.

Keyboard Functions

Caps Lock : The caps lock key is located on the left side of the keyboard right next to the "a" key. When this button is pressed, it makes every letter you type after that, appear in all capital letters like this: THIS IS AN EXAMPLE OF THE CAPS LOCK FUNCTION. It has no effect when typing numbers. They still will appear the same.

FN Key : The "fn" key is usually located at the bottom left of the keyboard but sometimes appears on the upper right hand side of the keyboard depending on the model. It usually has a white square around it or the letters may appear in a different color. Pressing and holding this key, while pressing another key that has either a corresponding white square on it or is the same color as the "fn" key, makes the computer do what is in the white square or in a different color. With some keyboards, this means being able to control the volume of the speakers or controlling the brightness of the screen all right from the keyboard.

Windows Symbol: On computers that have Microsoft Windows as an operating system, you may find the Windows symbol key on the bottom of the keyboard usually left in the bottom row. The key is marked with a symbol of four wavy squares and nothing else. Pressing this key will make the start menu appear, allowing you to having a starting place to navigate the computer's programs from when desired.

Arrow Keys : The arrow keys are usually located on the bottom right hand side of the keyboard. They allow the user to navigate one line up, down, or side to side in any given screen they may be working with. In a word processing program, it moves the cursor to a different place in the document corresponding with the arrow that was pressed. On the Internet, usually the up and down keys are only used to go up or down on the page.

F Keys: The very top of the keyboard is outlined with 12 keys numbered 1 to 12 with the letter "F" in front of the number. Each key will behave differently based on the program you are working with. Pressing "F1" will typically provide the user with a help menu for the given programme they are working on. In the search box of the help menu simply type in 'f keys' and it will show you the results of what each 'f' key will do in that programme . Many of these keys allow the user to navigate the computer without the use of a mouse.

Keyboard shortcut

Shortcut Keys	*Description*
Alt + F	File menu options in current program.
Alt + E	Edit options in current program
F1	Universal Help in almost every Windows program
Ctrl + A	Select all text
Ctrl + X	Cut selected item
Shift + Del	Cut selected item
Ctrl + C	Copy selected item
Ctrl + V	Paste
Shift + Ins	Pase
Home	Goes to beginning of current line
Ctrl + Home	Goes to beginning of document
End	Goes to end of current line
Ctrl + End	Goes to end of document
Shift + Home	Highlights from current position to beginning of line
Shift + End	Highlights from current position to end of line
Ctrl + Left arrow	Moves one word to the left at a time
Ctrl + Right arrow	Moves one word to the right at a time

Keyboard shortcut

Function	*Description*
F1	• Almost always used as the help key, almost every program will open the help screen when this key is pressed.

Function	Description
	• Windows Key + F1 would open the Microsoft Windows help and support center. • Open the Task Pane
F2	• In Windows commonly used to rename a highlighted icon or file. • Alt + Ctrl + F2 open a new document in Microsoft Word. • Ctrl + F2 display the print preview window in Microsoft Word.
F3	• Often opens a search feature for many programs including Microsoft Windows • Shift + F3 will change the text in Microsoft Word from upper to lower case or a capital letter at the beginning of every word
F4	• Open find window • Repeat the last action performed (Word 2000+) • Alt + F4 will close the program currently active in Microsoft Windows • Ctrl + F4 will close the open window within the current active window in Microsoft Windows
F5	• In all modern Internet browsers pressing F5 will refresh or reload the page or document window • Open the find, replace, and go to window in Microsoft Word • Starts a slideshow in PowerPoint
F6	• Move the cursor to the Address bar in Internet Explorer and Mozilla Firefox • Ctrl + Shift + F6 open to another open Microsoft Word document
F7	• Commonly used to spell check and grammar check a document in Microsoft

Function	*Description*
	programs such as Microsoft Word, Outlook, etc.
	• Shift + F7 runs a Thesaurus check on the word highlighted
F8	• Function key used to enter the Windows startup menu, commonly use to get into Windows Safe Mode
F9	• Open the Measurements toolbar in Quark 5.0.
F10	• In Microsoft Windows activates the menu bar of an open application.
	• Shift + F10 is the same as right-clicking on a highlighted icon, file, or Internet link.
F11	• Full-screen mode in all modern Internet browsers
F12	• Open the Save as window in Microsoft Word
	• Shift + F12 save the Microsoft Word document
	• Ctrl + Shift + F12 prints a document in Microsoft Word

INFORMATION AND COMMUNICATION TECHNOLOGY

Meaning and Definition of Information and Communication Technology

Information and Communication Technology is defined as the use of hardware and software for efficient management of information, i.e. storage, retrieval, processing, communication, diffusion and sharing of information for social, economical and cultural upliftment.

Information and Communication Technology (ICT) is defined as the implementation of different branches of technology in information and communication processing. In a broader sense, ICT is taken to refer to the whole set of enabling technology concerned with communication, manipulation of information (hardware and software), networking, data storage, transmission–encompassing data, voice and video.

The use of information and communication technologies in education makes teaching – learning process effective and interesting. To know the impact of ICT in education, we need to know two basic things: ICT, and education. The ***Information and Communication Technologies*** (ICT) is an umbrella term that includes any communication device or application, encompassing: radio, television, cellular phones, computer, and network hardware and software, satellite systems and so on, as well as the various services and applications associated with them, such as videoconferencing and distance learning. When such technologies are used for educational purposes, namely to support and improve the learning of students and to develop learning environments, ICT can be considered as a sub field of Educational Technology.

Education encompasses teaching and learning specific skills, and also something less tangible but more profound: the imparting of knowledge, positive judgment and well developed wisdom. Education has as one of its fundamental aspects the imparting of culture from generation to generation. Education means 'to draw out' facilitating realization of self potential and latent talents of an individual. It is an application of pedagogy, a body of theoretical and applied research relating to teaching and learning and draws on many disciplines such as psychology, philosophy, computer science, linguistics, neuroscience, sociology and anthropology. In view of ICT, education can be classified in three main categories- E-Learning, Blended Learning, and Distance Learning.

A. E-Learning: Electronic learning or e-learning is a general term used to refer to computer-enhanced learning. It is commonly associated with the field of advanced learning technology (ALT), which deals with both the technologies and associated methodologies in learning using networked and/or multimedia technologies. It is also known as ***online learning.*** Distance Education provided the base for e-learning's development. E-learning can be "on demand". It overcomes timing, attendance and travel difficulties.

B. Blended Learning: Blended Learning is the combination of multiple approaches to learning. It is usually used to define a situation where different delivery methods are combined together to deliver a particular course. These methods may include a mixture of face-to-face classrooms, self-paced learning and online classrooms as shown in below figure.

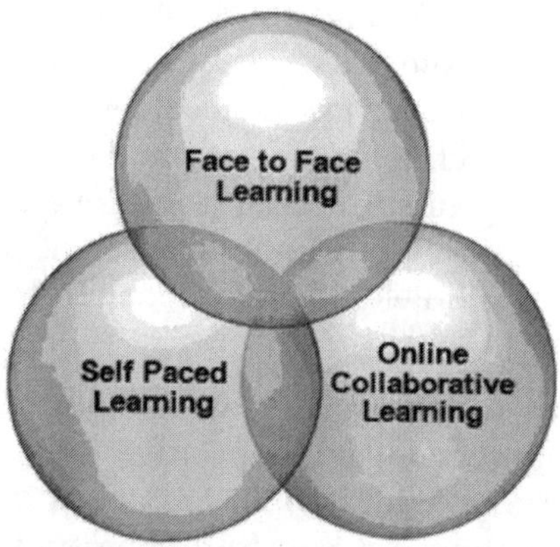

(a) ***Face to Face Learning:*** Face to face learning refers to learning that occurs in a traditional classroom setting where a faculty member delivers instruction to a group of learners. This could include lectures, workshops, presentations, tutoring, conference and much more.

(b) ***Self Paced Learning:*** Self paced learning provides the flexibility to learn according to the availability of learners' own time and pace, it occurs in a variety of ways such as: reading specific chapters from text book, studying course material presented through web-based or CD-based course, attending prerecorded

classes or sessions, reading articles referred by faculty member, working on assignments & projects and searching & browsing the internet.

(c) ***Online Collaborative Learning:*** Online collaboration involves interaction between learners and faculty members through the web; this interaction can occur in one of the following modes: Synchronous interaction and Asynchronous interaction

Synchronous, means "at the same time", it involves interacting with a faculty member and other learners via the Web in real time using technologies such as virtual classrooms and/ or chat rooms. On the other hand, Asynchronous means "not at the same time"; it enables learners to interact with their colleagues and faculty member at their own convenience; such as interacting through e-mail.

C. Distance Learning: It is a type of education, where students work on their own at home or at the office and communicate with faculty and other students via e-mail, electronic forums, videoconferencing, chat rooms, instant messaging and other forms of computer-based communication. It is also known as open learning. Most distance learning programs include a computer based training (CBT) system and communications tools to produce a virtual ***classroom.*** Because the Internet and World Wide Web are accessible from virtually all computer platforms, they serve as the foundation for many distance learning systems.

Aims of ICT

1. ICT was originally intended to serve as a means of improving efficiency in the educational process.
2. It can help to improve memory retention, increase motivation and gradually deepen understanding.
3. ICT can also be used to promote collaborative learning including role playing, group problem solving activities and articulated objects.

4. Generally ICT is promoting new approaches to working and learning and new ways of e-literacy.
5. ICT also changes the nature of motivation to learn.

Dimensions of Information and Communication Technology

Access to ICT and e-literacy has four primary dimensions: attitudinal, financial, skill and infrastructure.

1. ***Attitudinal:*** Perceiving ICT skills and access to the internet as value adding and important to future well being: perceiving the internet as having meaningful and relevant content: being confident and motivated to go online.
2. ***Financial:*** Being able to connect to the internet from home, work or a community location in a way, which enables a person to learn ICT skills and carry out required activities through affordable access to a PC with connectivity to the internet.
3. ***Skills:*** Having sufficient skills or access to tuition to develop and increase skills, to use ICT to an optimal level for personal and economic gain.
4. ***Infrastructure:*** Having sufficient levels of bandwidth available to carry out e-economic, e-government or educational interactions.

Objectives of ICT

(*a*) To create awareness about the use of Information and Communication Technologies (ICT) in Education.

(*b*) To familiarize with fundamental of ICT.

(*c*) To acquire knowledge of computers languages and software packages for education.

(*d*) To develop programming skills in computer languages for education.

(*e*) To develop skills in utilization of different software packages in education.

(*f*) To develop skills in utilizing intranet and internet.

(*g*) To utilize ICT for solving educational problems.

Educational Implications of ICT

(*a*) Time, space and socio-economic factors are no longer major barriers to learning.

(*b*) Decentralized nature of the new technology frees the learner from the technology provider.

(*c*) Learners have access to variety of learning resources.

(*d*) Up-to-date knowledge from any part of the world.

(*e*) New media allows interactive, learner need not be a passive recipient of knowledge.

(*f*) New technology allows the learner to receive information in a variety of formats.

Use of ICT from Academic Point of View

1. ***Students and ICT:*** The rapid technological development means that knowledge is no longer a "once in a life time" experiences for the individual. It is rather an asset, which constantly has to be updated. Therefore, the crucial new factor in connection with the information society is that students are to be qualified creatively to sort, select, process and use the get amount of information. Which ICT gives access to. Moreover, in connection with the basic education they are to acquire new methods of learning processes in order to enable them to take a material responsibility for a continual and lifelong updating their qualifications.

2. ***The teachers and ICT:*** The teachers are to be educated concurrently with the increase in the use of ICT. New knowledge based on the latest research and new interpretations of existing knowledge can in a few seconds be distributed globally with the use of information technology and electronic communication.

Knowledge is constantly changing or is becoming obsolete so rapidly that the distributors of knowledge-the teachers can hardly be constantly updated. Knowledge is not static but dynamic and it moves at lightening speed in the information society. The very speed in which the amount of knowledge is increasing globally makes other demands on the teachers of today and of the future. Therefore, it is necessary to revise the traditional understanding of the role of the teachers of today and of the future. Therefore, it is necessary to revise the traditional understanding of the role of the teacher in the information society's education system.

3. ***The subjects and ICT:*** When we speak colloquially about the integration of ICT in education and teaching, we speak primarily about the ICT-integration in the subjects (and the teaching/dissemination of them). It is, therefore, a crucial question, whether the integration of ICT has bearings on the self-understanding and development of a subject and if it has, which ones and to what extent.
4. ***Equal and flexible access to lifelong education:*** Regardless of age, educational background and geographical location, it is to be ensured that everybody have the opportunity of participation in a wide range of educational activities. An ICT educational policy strategy in this area among other things include a strong development of virtual educational programmes where physical presence is not imperative and here the advantage of programmes, which are independent of geography and time, can be implemented. There are already numbers of programmers within adult education, but in the future, there ought to be an additional focus on increasing the ICT-qualifications of the entire population.
5. ***Coordination of ICT-related research and education:*** There is a need for strengthening of the research effort within

education and teaching methods in general, including a special effort within the new ICT-based education and teaching methods. In that way, a systematic gathering and development of new pioneering education and teaching methods will be ensured.

Stages of Teaching and Learning with ICT

Teaching and learning process is always going together; we cannot consider these two as separate and independent activities. In fact, these are similar as two sides of the same coin, interconnected and interrelated. The process of teaching and learning in institutes around the world can be divided into four main stages. These four stages are shown in Figure.

Stage 1 Discovering ICT tools

Stage 2 Learning how to use ICT tools

Stage 3 Understanding how and when to use ICT tools to achieve particular purposes

Stage 4 Specializing in the use of ICT tools

Stage 1 - Discovering ICT tools: This stage focuses on discovery of new ICT tools by teachers and students. This is linked with the emerging approach in ICT development.

Stage 2 – Learning how to use ICT tools: This stage emphasizes on learning the use of new ICT tools. It involves the use of general or particular applications of ICT.

Stage 3 – Understanding how and when to use ICT tools: It focuses on understanding how and when to use ICT tools to achieve a particular purpose, such as in completing a given project. This stage indicates the ability to recognize situations where ICT will be helpful, choosing the most appropriate tools for a particular task, and using these tools in combination to solve real problems.

Stage 4 – Specializing in the use of ICT tools: The fourth and last stage involves specializing in the use of ICT tools. This requires deep knowledge about using ICT tools. In this stage students study ICT as a subject to become specialists. Such study concerns vocational or professional education rather than general education.

INTEGRATION OF ICT IN TEACHING AND LEARNING

World over, educational institutions are under pressure to integrate information and communication Technology (ICT) with teaching, learning, evaluation, research, administrations and professional development. This increased emphasis is justified considering the knowledge, skills, and competencies required by the young generation to survive in an increasingly sophisticated technological world. Undoubtedly, ICT has brought about many challenges and opportunities for education. The educational system needs to come to terms with these new challenges and take full advantage of the opportunities. If educational institutions have to ensure that their students leave the institutions as confident individuals capable of using new technology creatively and productively then their teachers should have the competence to integrate the emerging technologies and the digital content with all their operations.

Steps to Integrate ICT

In school level, Integrating Information and Communication Technology in Teaching-Learning Process involves in the following steps:

1. ***Awareness:*** To instruct and creating awareness of Information and communication technology among teachers.
2. ***Fundamental Knowledge:*** To create and insert the basic knowledge of the modern technology those are involved in teaching and learning towards teachers. The basic knowledges are (*a*) Nature of Media, (*b*) Use of Media in teaching learning process and (*c*) implementing the media in teaching.
3. ***Proper Training:*** It is needed to give proper training to teachers about the equipment and instrument, which are utilized and involved in teaching.

4. ***Implementation/Put into Practice:*** After receiving the training, the teachers should implement his training in his teaching and evaluation.
5. ***Follow-up Activities:*** While implementing new technology, there may so many difficulties and experiments arise. These may be eradicated through sharing and consulting the expert.

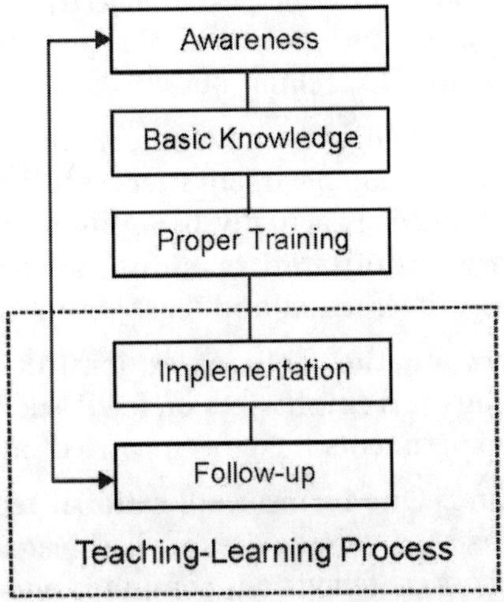

Integrating Educational Technology in School Education

Educational technology developed as a new subject in the field of education during the last few years. The term 'Education' includes teaching, learning, instruction and training. In schools, Educational Technology has its application in the following general working areas:

1. *Curriculum Construction*: In the present technological and psychological age, the application of scientific and technological knowledge is much essential for the curriculum construction. The curriculum construction has become a very tedious job in the field of education. It can be simplified with the help of educational technology.

2. ***Selection of Teaching-Learning Strategies:*** The selection of teaching-learning strategies turns easy with the help of educational technology.
3. ***Selection of Audio-Visual Material***: Another important working area of educational technology is that the teacher can select easily the audio-visual aids with its assistance.
4. ***Determination of Educational Objectives***: The software aspect of educational technology contributes in the formulation of teaching objectives.
5. ***Teachers Training***: The new innovations in educational technology can be used successfully in teachers' training and it is actually being done, such as micro-teaching, stimulated teaching, system approach, classroom interaction and teaching models etc.
6. ***Feedback***: In the field of education, educational technology has emphasizes on feedback for evaluation. Many experiments have been carried out in the area.
7. ***Hardwares***: One form of educational technology also occurs as hardware devices such as teaching machines, tape-recorder, television, computer and satellite. The learning in the classroom can be made effective with their use.

Opportunities of Integrating ICTs in Education

Modern universities and institutes have a mission to make teaching learning process effective and interesting. Study of use of ICTs in education, reveals the following opportunities:

A. Improved Teaching-Learning Process: The traditional way of teaching learning process can be made more effective and interesting by using information and communication technologies. For example, when a teacher uses audio, video, or power point presentations in his/her lecture, the whole class becomes more attentive about the lecture. Such activities also help students to understand the things easily.

B. Increased Availability of Study Material: In traditional learning system, students and teachers are limited to get knowledge on a particular topic through printed materials only. But use of ICT facilitates them to get variety of study materials on a particular topic using internet from anywhere and anytime.

C. Support for Distance Education and E-Learning: The use of ICT supports distance education and e-learning. Each of the different ICTs - prints, audio/video cassettes, radio and TV broadcasts, computers or the Internet may be used for this purpose. There is a minor difference between distance education and e-learning. The use of ICTs is higher in e-learning than distance learning.

D. Improved Admission and Examination Process: Using ICTs universities and institutes can improve the admission process by putting admission form online and receiving completed form online. They can also generate admit cards for entrance examination online. Even they can conduct entrance and semester/ annual examination online. This will speed up admission and examination process. It also helps in faster result declaration.

E. Help in Research Activities: Application of ICT in education enriches the research activities. Researchers can get information about recent developments in different segments, collect variety of information on a particular topic, and can generate innovative ideas and new findings. Using appropriate software we can easily calculate complex calculations and generate variety of graphs.

Challenges in Integrating ICTs in Education

While considering the opportunities associated with ICTenhanced education it can be said that ICT-enhanced education is better than a simple education, but there are many challenges, which hamper the exploration and exploitation of its opportunities. In view of integrating ICTs in education have following key challenges:

(A) ICT Infrastructure: The main challenge for ICT-enhanced education is the availability of information and communication technologies infrastructure. Before any ICT-based programme is launched, policymakers and planners must ensure the availability of the followings: appropriate rooms or buildings to house the technology, computers as well as affordable Internet service for on line learning, and availability of electricity and telephony. In developing countries large areas are still without a reliable supply of electricity and the nearest telephones are miles away.

(B) Language and Content: English is the dominant language of the Internet. An estimated 80 percent of online content is in English. A large proportion of the educational software produced in the world market is in English. For developing countries in the Asia- Pacific where English language proficiency is not high, especially outside metropolitan areas, this represents a serious barrier in maximizing the educational benefits of the World Wide Web. Even in countries such as Philippines, Malaysia, Singapore, and India where English is a second language; it is desirable that teaching and learning materials, preferably be developed in the local languages.

(C) Teachers with ICT Skills: Lack of teachers equipped with ICT skills is another problem for the use of ICT in education. The institutes where ICT is going to be integrated in education, first of all their teachers must be well trained about ICT tools in education. Before going to teach to students, teachers must know about how and when to use ICT tools to achieve particular purposes.

(D) Change Management: Managing the change is one of the biggest problems, as teachers don't want to accept change easily. Change management issues must be addressed as new work practices, new ways of processing and performing tasks are introduced. In general a large number of teachers in educational institutes are non ICT proficient, and resistance to change. Research has shown that the strategy of adding technology to the already existing activities in institutes and in the classroom, without changing habitual teaching practices, does not produce good results in student learning. The reason for this is due to the fact that the vast majority of teachers are not proficient users of technology, especially computer technology. A number of studies have shown that most teachers consider the two main obstacles to using technology in pedagogical practices to be a lack of resources and training.

(E) Leadership: Integrating ICT in education is not an easy task, as it requires a wide range of support including higher management, and teachers. Therefore it is necessary to properly convince them for their support, and for this task a leader is required. Leadership is necessary before, during and after project implementation. Before the project is initiated, leadership is needed in order to explain the model, the concept and create awareness; during the project, leadership is needed to manage change and support the project; and after the project, it is needed to pledge the required adaptability and flexibility of the initiative.

ICT APPLICATIONS

Word Processor

Word processor (more formally known as document preparation system) is a computer application used for the production (including composition, editing, formatting, and possibly printing) of any sort of printable material. Word processor may also refer to a type of stand-alone office machine, popular in the 1970s and 1980s, combining the keyboard text-entry and printing functions of an electric typewriter with a dedicated processor (like a computer processor) for the editing of text. Although features and design varied between manufacturers and models, with new features added as technology advanced, word processors for several years usually featured a monochrome display and the ability to save documents on memory cards or diskettes. Later models introduced innovations such as spell-checking programs, increased formatting options, and dot-matrix printing. As the more versatile combination of a personal computer and separate printer became commonplace, most business-machine companies stopped manufacturing the word processor as a stand-alone office machine. Word processors are descended from early ***text formatting*** tools (sometimes called ***text justification*** tools, from their only real capability). Word processing was one of the earliest applications for the personal computer in office productivity.

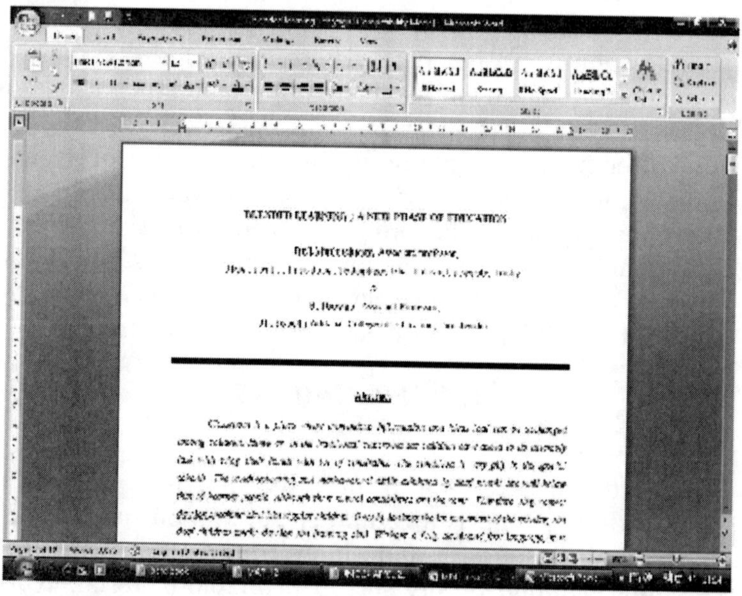

Microsoft Word is the most widely used word processing software. Microsoft estimates that over 500,000,000 people use the Microsoft Office suite, which includes Word. Many other word processing applications exist, including WordPerfect (which dominated the market from the mid-1980s to early-1990s on computers running Microsoft's MS-DOS operating system) and open source applications OpenOffice.org Writer, AbiWord, KWord, and LyX. Web-based word processors, such as Google Docs, are a relatively new category.

Characteristic of Word Processors

Word processing typically implies the presence of text manipulation functions that extend beyond a basic ability to enter and change text, such as automatic generation of:

- batch mailings using a form letter template and an address database (also called mail merging);
- indices of keywords and their page numbers;
- tables of contents with section titles and their page numbers;
- tables of figures with caption titles and their page numbers;
- cross-referencing with section or page numbers;
- footnote numbering;
- New versions of a document using variables (e.g. model numbers, product names, etc.)

Other word processing functions include "spell checking" (actually checks against wordlists), "grammar checking" (checks for what seem to be simple grammar errors), and a "thesaurus" function (finds words with similar or opposite meanings). Other common features include collaborative editing, comments and annotations, support for images and diagrams and internal cross-referencing.

Application of Word Processors

Using a computer to create, edit, and print documents. Of all computer applications, word processing is the most common. To perform word processing, you need a computer, a special program called a ***word processor***, and a printer. A word processor enables you to create a document, store it electronically on a disk, display it on a screen, modify it by entering commands and characters from the keyboard, and print it on a printer.

The great advantage of word processing over using a typewriter is that you can make changes without retyping the entire document. If you make a typing mistake, you simply back up the cursor and correct your mistake. If you want to delete a paragraph, you simply remove it, without leaving a trace. It is equally easy to insert a word, sentence, or paragraph in the middle of a document. Word processors also make it easy to move sections of text from one place to another within a document, or between documents. When you have made all the changes you want, you can send the file to a printer to get a hardcopy.

Word processors vary considerably, but all word processors support the following basic features:

- Insert text: Allows you to insert text anywhere in the document.
- Delete text: Allows you to erase characters, words, lines, or pages as easily as you can cross them out on paper.
- Cut and paste: Allows you to remove (*cut*) a section of text from one place in a document and insert (*paste*) it somewhere else.
- Copy : Allows you to duplicate a section of text.
- Page size and margins: Allows you to define various page sizes and margins, and the word processor will automatically readjust the text so that it fits.
- Search and replace : Allows you to direct the word processor to search for a particular word or phrase. You can also direct the word processor to replace one group of characters with another everywhere that the first group appears.
- Word wrap : The word processor automatically moves to the next line when you have filled one line with text, and it will readjust text if you change the margins.
- Print: Allows you to send a document to a printer to get hardcopy.

Word processors that support only these features (and maybe a few others) are called ***text editors***. Most word processors, however, support additional features that enable you to manipulate and format documents in more sophisticated ways. These more advanced word processors are sometimes called ***full-featured word processors.*** Full-featured word processors usually support the following features or uses of word processor.

- File management : Many word processors contain file management capabilities that allow you to create, delete, move, and search for files.
- Font specifications: Allows you to change fonts within a document. For example, you can specify bold, italics, and underlining. Most word processors also let you change the font size and even the typeface.
- Footnotes and cross-references: Automates the numbering and placement of footnotes and enables you to easily cross-reference other sections of the document.
- Graphics: Allows you to embed illustrations and graphs into a document. Some word processors let you create the illustrations within the word processor; others let you insert an illustration produced by a different program.
- Headers, footers and page numbering: Allows you to specify customized headers and footers that the word processor will put at the top and bottom of every page. The word processor automatically keeps track of page numbers so that the correct number appears on each page.
- Layout : Allows you to specify different margins within a single document and to specify various methods for indenting paragraphs.
- Macros : A ***macro*** is a character or word that represents a series of keystrokes. The keystrokes can represent

text or commands. The ability to define macros allows you to save yourself a lot of time by replacing common combinations of keystrokes.

- Merges: Allows you to merge text from one file into another file. This is particularly useful for generating many files that have the same format but different data. Generating mailing labels is the classic example of using merges.
- Spell checker : A utility that allows you to check the spelling of words. It will highlight any words that it does not recognize.
- Tables of contents and indexes: Allows you to automatically create a table of contents and index based on special codes that you insert in the document.
- Thesaurus: A built-in thesaurus that allows you to search for synonyms without leaving the word processor.
- Windows : Allows you to edit two or more documents at the same time. Each document appears in a separate ***window***. This is particularly valuable when working on a large project that consists of several different files.
- ***WYSIWYG (what you see is what you get):*** With WYSIWYG, a document appears on the display screen exactly as it will look when printed.

Spread Sheets

A spreadsheet is a sheet of paper that shows accounting or other data in rows and columns; a spreadsheet is also a computer application program that simulates a physical spreadsheet by capturing, displaying, and manipulating data arranged in rows and columns. The spreadsheet is one of the most popular uses of the personal computer. In a spreadsheet, spaces that hold items of data are called cells. Each cell is labeled according to its placement (for example, A1, A2, A3...) and may have an absolute or relative reference to the cells around it. A spreadsheet is generally designed to hold numerical data and short text strings. Spreadsheets usually provide the ability to portray data relationships graphically. Spreadsheets generally do not offer the ability to structure and label data items as fully as a database and usually do not offer the ability to query the database. In general, a spreadsheet is a much simpler program than a database program.

Daniel Bricklin and Bob Frankston created the first spreadsheet application, VisiCalc (for "visible calculator"). Lotus 1-2-3 came next, followed by Microsoft Excel. While Lotus 1-2-3 was the first to introduce cell names and macros, Microsoft Excel implemented a graphical user interface and the ability to point and click using a mouse. There are many other spreadsheet applications on the market today; however, Lotus 1-2-3 and Microsoft Excel continue to be the most popular.

Microsoft Excel

Microsoft had been developing Excel on the Macintosh platform for several years at this point, where it had developed into a fairly powerful system. A port of Excel to Windows 2.0 resulted in a fully functional Windows spreadsheet. The more robust Windows 3.x platforms of the early 1990s made it possible for Excel to take market share from Lotus. By the time Lotus responded with usable Windows products, Microsoft had started compiling their Office suite. Starting in the mid 1990s continuing through the present, Microsoft Excel has dominated the commercial electronic spreadsheet market.

Features of Spread Sheet

Cells: A "cell" can be thought of as a box for holding a datum. A single cell is usually referenced by its column and row (A2 would represent the cell below containing the value

10). Usually rows are referenced in decimal notation starting from 1, while columns use 26-adic bijective numeration using the letters A-Z as numerals. Its physical size can usually be tailored for its content by dragging its height or width at box intersections (or for entire columns or rows by dragging the column or rows headers). An array of cells is called a "sheet" or "worksheet".

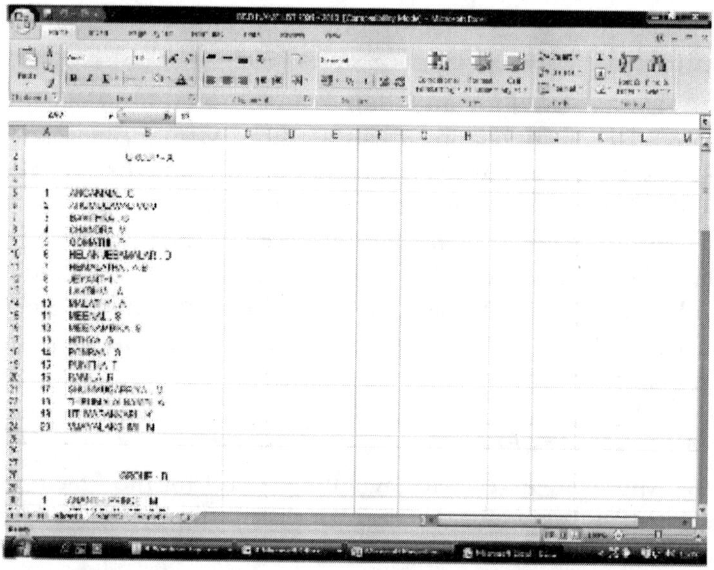

Values: A value can be entered from the computer keyboard by directly typing into the cell itself. Alternatively, a value can be based on a formula (see below), which might perform a calculation, display the current date or time, or retrieve external data such as a stock quote or a database value. The Spreadsheet *Value Rule* Computer scientist Alan Kay used the term *value rule* to summarize a spreadsheet's operation: a cell's value relies solely on the formula the user has typed into the cell.

Automatic recalculation: A standard of spreadsheets since the middle 80s, this optional feature eliminates the need to manually request the spreadsheet program to recalculate values (nowadays typically the default option unless specifically 'switched off' for large spreadsheets, usually to improve performance). Some earlier spreadsheets required a manual request to recalculate, since recalculation of large or complex spreadsheets often reduced data entry speed. Many modern spreadsheets still retain this option.

Real-time update: This feature refers to updating a cell's contents periodically when its value is derived from an external source - such as a cell in another "remote" spreadsheet. For shared, web-based spreadsheets, it applies to "immediately" updating cells that have been altered by another user. All dependent cells have to be updated also.

Locked cell: Once entered, selected cells (or the entire spreadsheet) can optionally be "locked" to prevent accidental overwriting. Typically this would apply to cells containing formulas but might be applicable to cells containing "constants" such as a kilogram/pounds conversion factor (2.20462262 to eight decimal places). Even though individual cells are marked as locked, the spreadsheet data is not protected until the feature is activated in the file preferences.

Data format: A cell or range can optionally be defined to specify how the value is displayed. The default display format is usually set by its initial content if not specifically previously set, so that for example "31/12/2007" or "31 Jan 2007" would default to the cell format of "date". Similarly adding a % sign after a numeric value would tag the cell as a percentage cell format. The cell contents are not changed by this format, only the displayed value.

Cell formatting: Depending on the capability of the spreadsheet application, each cell (like its counterpart the "style" in a word processor) can be separately formatted using the attributes of either the content (font size, color, bold or italic) or the cell (border thickness, background shading, and color). To aid the readability of a spreadsheet, cell formatting may be conditionally applied to data - for example, a negative number may be displayed in red.

Cell reference: In place of a named cell, an alternative approach is to use a cell (or grid) reference. Most cell references indicate another cell in the same spreadsheet, but a cell reference can also refer to a cell in a different sheet within the same spreadsheet, or (depending on the implementation) to a cell in another spreadsheet entirely, or to a value from a remote application. A typical cell reference in "A1" style consists of one or two case-insensitive letters to identify the column (if there are up to 256 columns: A-Z and AA-IV) followed by a row number (e.g. in the range 1-65536).

Cell ranges: Likewise, instead of using a named range of cells, a range reference can be used. Reference to a range of cells is typically of the form (A1:A6) which specifies all the cells in the range A1 through to A6. A formula such as "=SUM (A1:A6)" would add all the cells specified and put the result in the cell containing the formula itself.

Sheets: In the earliest spreadsheets, cells were a simple two-dimensional grid. Over time, the model has been expanded to include a third dimension, and in some cases a series of named grids, called sheets. The most advanced examples allow inversion and rotation operations which can slice and project the data set in various ways.

Formulas: Animation of a simple spreadsheet that multiplies values in the left column by 2 then sums the calculated values from the right column to the bottom-most cell. In this example, only the values in the A column are entered (10, 20, 30), and the remainder of cells are formulas. Formulas in the B column multiply values from the A column using relative references, and the formula in B4 uses the SUM () function to find the sum of values in the B1:B3 range. A formula identifies the calculation needed to place the result in the cell it is contained within. A cell containing a formula therefore has two display components; the formula itself and the resulting value. The formula is normally only shown when the cell is selected by "clicking" the mouse over a particular cell; otherwise it contains the result of the calculation.

Remote spreadsheet: Whenever a reference is made to a cell or group of cells that are not located within the current physical spreadsheet file, it is considered as accessing a "remote" spreadsheet. The contents of the referenced cell may be accessed either on first reference with a manual update or more recently in the case of web based spreadsheets, as a near real time value with a specified automatic refresh interval.

Charts : Many spreadsheet applications permit charts, graphs or histograms to be generated from specified groups of cells which are dynamically re-built as cell contents change. The generated graphic component can either be embedded within the current sheet or added as a separate object.

Applications of Spread Sheet

Spreadsheets are typically used by teachers to keep track of teaching. The most well-known spreadsheets are Microsoft's Excel, Lotus 1-2-3 and WordPerfect's Quattro. Spreadsheets are one of the most underrated programs in an office suite. Their use goes far beyond creating simple expense sheets and employee time sheets, as spreadsheets are complex programs offering a range of powerful features, including game programming, text effects, graphing and graphics capabilities.

Budget Planning: A spreadsheet is an excellent budget planning tool, with calculation features that make keeping track of expenses and income easy, and calculating end-of-year data a breeze. Every year the administrator should plan the budget through spreadsheet. Budget planning consists of staff's salary, expenses in building construction and purchasing library books.

Charts: Spreadsheets include graphic capabilities that allow you to calculate and compile information into visual representations. This is a great way to keep track of an students passing record or any other information that needs to be tracked and calculated on a regular basis. Teacher can identify the student's level through chart application in spread sheet.

Database and Address Books: A spreadsheet can be a versatile database, keeping track of important web pages and names, numbers and addresses of students and staff contacts. It can even be used as a reference database for staff. All the students' information is stored in spread sheet. It is very useful for communication purpose. Student's personal record also entered in to spreadsheet.

Surveys: You can use a spreadsheet to take surveys. Simply enter the survey results and use the calculation features to analyze and sort the information. You do a educational project and calculation through spreadsheet applications.

Power Point Presentation

Another important category of educational computing is the use of innovative instructional software. There are several software programmes that are available for classroom teaching/presentation. Special mention has to be made on the use of "PowerPoint" presentation" in classroom teaching. PowerPoint is the presentation software used to create slides, handouts and speaker notes.

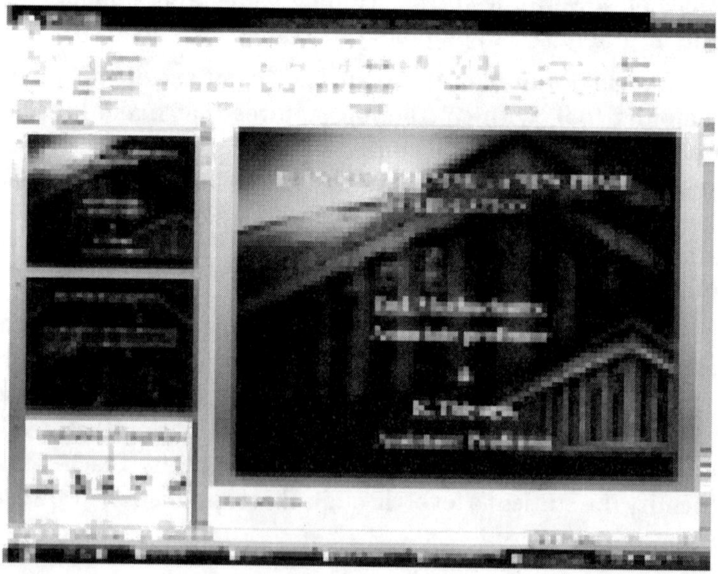

PowerPoint helps the user to prepare, update and order slide-based presentation material quickly. Slide means one page of power point presentation. The slide size can be set to the size of transparent sheet, a 35 mm film or the actual computer screen. The slides prepared can be printed on plain paper or on transparent sheet and displayed on computer screen, multimedia projector or through film projector. PowerPoint presentation has a sequence of slides and each slide may contain objects such as text, picture, chart, table and other types of multimedia elements. Slides can have title text and body text. The title text provides title for each slide and body text consists of a series of main and sub-points referred by bullets.

Features of Power Point Presentation

Power Point incorporates the following features which make its superior to the other presentation methods.

1. ***Slider Transition :*** A transition is how PowerPoint gets from one slide to the next slide during presentation. The usual method of removing the previous slide and putting the next one is very boring. Power-Point enables the user to assign 45 different special effects to each slide transition. For example by mouse click or automatic time setting, the slides can be displayed one by one. Moreover, if any part of the slide is to be hidden temporarily, provisions are available to perform such things.

2. ***Color Schemes and Fonts :*** PowerPoint supports colour schemes and fonts. User can select a pre-designed color or form a new color scheme as he desires by picking from among the 16 million colors. In addition, different colors can be set for each object like Title Text, Body Text, and Background etc. PowerPoint enables the user to project individual characters in different ways. It supports all the MS Word font styles and font sizes. Using them, the user can dress up his presentation materials and make the text appear in different styles.

3. ***Auto Layout and Masters :*** PowerPoint has a number of Auto Layout choices of common slide making tasks. These layouts have text boxes, places to insert pictures, bullet list, formatting and so on. Auto Layout takes care of things like margin, line spacing etc. Auto Layout helps the user to design each slide effectively in an easier manner. Masters specify common design elements that the user wishes to include throughout his presentation. PowerPoint comes with a variety of predefined masters and they contain elements like backgrounds, font choices, color schemes, logos etc.
4. ***Adding Pictures :*** PowerPoint is well equipped to add all sorts of pictures like clip art, drawings, graphs, and charts. Power point comes with more than 1000 clip art pictures that the user can take directly add into his presentation. Common graphics operations like moving, sizing, shading, boxing and stretching can be applied on these pictures. Other photo images and scanned images can also be included into slides if the user wants.
5. ***Adding Charts :*** Power point enables the user to illustrate a point with a chart (e.g. Bar Chart, Pie Chart etc.,). The graph, which works within Power Point, helps the user to create and edit a Chart. These charts can be added into a slide by choosing the appropriate slide layouts. There are 14 basic types of chart. The chart type can be changed at any time without changing the chart data.
6. ***Drawing on Slides :*** Drawing is a tedious work and it consumes a lot of time. Power Point has powerful drawing tools like Corel Draw. It has tools for drawing basic shapes such as line, circle, arc, square etc.
7. ***Equation, Word Art and other Ornaments :*** For mathematical work, Power point comes with an equation editor. The Word Art program of MS Word

can be used from PowerPoint, which transforms an ordinary text into text arts. In addition tree like charts (hierarchical chart) and Microsoft Excel worksheets can be easily added into Power Point slides to make more efficient presentation.

8. ***Adding Multimedia Effects :*** Multimedia effects like sound, animated picture and video clips can be inserted into PowerPoint slides.
9. ***Other Common Windows Features :*** PowerPoint is a window application software and supports all common Windows Features like
   - Graphical User Interface
   - Keyboard and Mouse Operation
   - Special Character
   - MS Word Editing features like cut, paste, etc
   - Dialog Boxers and Message Boxes

Total PowerPoint is user friendly presentation software which helps to design presentation material beautifully even if the user is not an art designer.

Power Point Presentation as a Method of Teaching

Teacher can be followed the following steps for implementing the Power point Presentation in his classroom

1. Selection: A Teacher can select the power point slide in the following manner :

- The Slide should be attractive to the students.
- The slide should be made according to the teacher and the student's interaction.
- The slide should be explaining the concept of lesson in clearly.

2. Preview:

- The teacher should see the slides before the presentation.

- *The* teacher should to know whether the students able to understand the slides.
- If the teacher having a workbook for the lesson then he should read the explanation about the topic before going to the presentation.
- The teacher should see the slides before the presentation and must to prepare for motivating the students.
- The teacher should give the related assignment task to the student before presenting the lesson.

3. Preparation:

- The teacher should know the audience, equipment, and presentation room.
- The teacher should begin with a joke or story or greeting.
- The teacher should move around to focus attention on you. Remain still to focus attention on your slides.
- The teacher should give the small introduction about lesson and then start the presentation

4. Presentation:

- The teacher should correct the equipment (like LCD, computer) and display the picture presentation clearly.
- The teacher should interact with the student in the middle of the Presentation.
- The teacher should display the slides in the sequential order.
- If it is necessary to take the notes. The teacher should allow the students to take the notes, during presentation.

5. Follow-up Activities:

- Teacher should write the preview of the lesson in the block board

- Teacher should made a conversation to the students after the completion of power point presentation
- Teacher should ask the question to the students for knowing the achievement level of students about the content presented.
- Teacher should create the opportunity for going field trips and research work to the students.
- Teacher should give a assignment and homework to the student.

Advantages of Power Point Presentation

Power point is best suited for :

- Organizing and reorganizing information efficiently so that students see the structure of a classroom teaching session.
- Providing more time for listening and comprehending so that class time is used effectively
- Illustrating concepts with pictures and other multimedia
- Merging text, graphics, sound, multimedia, offering control and visual dynamics
- Allowing the teacher easily to modify/enhance slides and lecture notes
- Allowing the teacher to face the students (rather than facing the blackboard)
- Presenting outlines of information in a sequential manner

ICT FOR RESEARCH:

On-line Journals/ e-Journals

The emergence of information and communication technology has made a tremendous impact on education. One of the important developments is the electronic journals popularly known as e-journals. Many of these journals are operated with no fee at all or else with submission fee paid by authors and thus freely accessible. The electronic serials may be defined very broadly as any journal, magazine, e'zine, webzine, newsletter or type of electronic serial publication, which is available over the internet. All modern electronic journals are mostly available via the web. Many organizations and publications are publishing e-journals. Some of the large e-journal publishers are listed below.

An electronic journal (or electronic serial) is an electronic publication that may be available via the web or email by subscription or free of charge. Electronic journals can be born digital with no print equivalent or can exist as an online version of a print journal. Issues for the preservation of electronic journals include the differing interests of the stakeholders - publishers, libraries, authors and the researchers that utilise the publications; costs and funding issues, such as fees for access; licensing and copyright issues, such as who can access them and when.

Type of E-Journals: basically the e-journals are grouped into two categories, which are as follows:

- Electronic journals along with print version.
- 'Electronic only' journals of which again there are two types: one available by fee and the other freely accessible.

Features of e-journals:

- Electronic journals have a number of salient features over the print version. These salient features are listed here under:
- The speed of publication and delivery of each of e-journals and articles is much faster than print, further reducing the gap between author of the paper and the end user.
- Internet has demonstrated that besides photograph and other images, video and audio based journals can also be delivered using the appropriate hardware and

software. Many of the educational e-journals having all these features are not available over the internet.

- E-journals provides the facilities of downloading, printing the appropriate articles at the end user workstation.
- E-journals provide links to the related articles cited in each article and other useful resources.
- The conservation and preservation problem will be minimum with e-journals compared to the print journals.
- Cost involved in publishing and distributing of e-journals will be less than print.

e-books

An e-book (short for electronic book and also known as a digital book, ebook and eBook) is "a portable electronic device used to download and read books or magazines that are in digital form." Sometimes the equivalent of a conventional printed book, e-books can also be born digital. The ***Oxford Dictionary of English*** defines the e-book as "an electronic version of a printed book," but e-books can and do exist without any print equivalent. E-books are usually read on dedicated hardware devices known as ***e-Readers*** or ***e-book devices.*** Personal computers and some cell phones can also be used to read e-books.

An ebook is an electronic (or digital) version of a book. The term is used ambiguously to refer to either an individual work in a digital format, or a hardware device used to read books in digital format. Some users deprecate the second meaning in favour of the more precise "ebook device". Though e-texts are available as digitally encoded books and the term is often used synonymously with the term ***ebook***, that usage is deprecated. The term e-text is used for the more limited case of data in ASCII text format, while the more general e-book can be in a specialized (and, at times, proprietary) file format. An ebook is commonly bundled by a publisher for distribution (as an ebook, an ezine, or a internet newspaper), whereas e-text is distributed in ASCII (or plain text). Metadata relating to the text is sometimes included with etext (though it appears more frequently with ebooks).

E-book Advantages

- *Availability:* Mobile availability of e-books may be provided for users with a mobile data connection, so that these e-books need not be stored on the device. An e-book can be offered indefinitely, without ever going "out of print".
- *Portability and Storage:* In the space that a comparably sized print book takes up, an e-reader can potentially contain thousands of e-books, limited only by its memory capacity. If space is at a premium, such as in a backpack or at home, it can be an advantage that an e-book collection takes up little room or weight.
- *Language Accessibility:* E-book websites can include the ability to translate books into many different languages, making the works available to speakers of languages not covered by printed translations.
- *E-Reader Attributes:* Depending on the device, an e-book may be readable in low light or even total darkness. Many newer readers have the ability to display motion, enlarge or change fonts, use Text-to-speech software to read the text aloud, search for key

terms, find definitions, or allow highlighting bookmarking and annotation.

- *Costs:* While an e-book reader costs much more than one book, the electronic texts are generally cheaper. Moreover, a great share of books are available free of charge. E-books can be printed for less than the price of traditional new books using new on-demand book printers.
- *Security:* Depending on possible digital rights management, e-books can be backed up to recover them in the case of loss or damage and it may be possible to recover a new copy without cost from the distributor.
- *Distribution:* Compared to print publishing, it is cheaper and easier for authors to self-publish e-books. Also, the dispersal of a free e-book copy can stimulate the sales of the printed version. An e-book can be purchased, downloaded, and used immediately, whereas when one buys a book one has to go to a bookshop, or wait for a delivery.
- *Environmental Concerns:* The production of e-books does not consume paper, ink, etc. Printed books use 3 times more raw materials and 78 times more water to produce albeit they do not require a machine for use

Drawbacks

- *Availability of Works:* Not all books are available as e-books.
- *Changing Technologies:* Ebook formats and file types continue to develop and change through time through advances and developments in technology or the introduction of new proprietary formats. While printed books remain readable for many years, e-books may need to be copied or converted to a new carrier or file type over time.

- ***Aesthetic Appeal:*** Paper books can be bought and wrapped for a present and a library of books can provide visual appeal, while the digital nature of e-books makes them non-visible or tangible. E-books cannot provide the physical feel of the cover, paper, and binding of the original printed work.
- ***Power and Shelf Life:*** A book will never turn off and would be unusable only if damaged or after many decades. The shelf life of a printed book exceeds that of an e-book reader, as over time the reader's battery will drain and require recharging.
- ***Durability:*** E-book readers are more susceptible to damage from being dropped or hit than a print book. Due to faults in hardware or software, e-book readers may malfunction and data loss can occur. As with any piece of technology, the reader must be protected from the elements (such as extreme cold, heat, water, etc.), while print books are not susceptible to damage from electromagnetic pulses, surges, impacts, or extreme temperatures.
- ***Artistry and Author's Vision:*** An author who publishes a book often puts more into the work than simply the words on the pages. E-books may cause people "to do the grazing and quick reading that screens enable, rather than be by themselves with the author's ideas." They may use the e-books simply for reference purposes rather than reading for pleasure and leisure.
- ***Costs:*** The cost of an e-book reader far exceeds that of a single book, and e-books often cost the same as their print versions. Due to the high cost of the initial investment in some form of e-reader, e-books are cost prohibitive to much of the world's population.
- ***Security:*** Because of the high-tech appeal of the e-reader, they are a greater target for theft than an individual print book. Along with the theft of the physical device, any e-books it contains also become

stolen. if an e-book is stolen, accidentally lost, or deleted, in the absence of a backup it may have to be repurchased.

- *Limitations of Readers:* The screen resolutions of reading devices are currently lower than actual printed materials. Because of proprietary formats or lack of file support, formatted e-books may be unusable on certain readers.
- *Environmental Concerns:* E-book readers require various toxic substances to produce, are non-biodegradable, and the disposal of their batteries in particular raises environmental concerns. As technologies rapidly change and old devices become obsolete, there will be larger amounts of toxic wastes that are not easily biodegradable like paper.
- *Privacy Concerns:* E books and software can easily track data, times, usage, pages, and details about what one is reading and how often. Similar to this is the growing amount of data available through Google search engines, Face book, and through data mining. For the first time in history it is now far easier to track and record what specific people might be reading. The notions of privacy, private writing, solitude, and personal reading are changing.
- *Picture Books:* Books with large pictures (such as children's books) or diagrams are more inconvenient for viewing and reading.

Courseware

Courseware is educational material intended as kits for teachers or trainers or as tutorials for students, usually packaged for use with a computer. Courseware can encompass any knowledge area, but information technology subjects are most common. Courseware is frequently used for delivering education about the personal computer and its most popular business applications, such as word processing and spreadsheet programs. Courseware is also widely used in information technology industry certification programs, such as the Microsoft Certified Systems Engineer (MCSE) and the Computing Technology Industry Associaton's A+ examination. The CD-ROM is the most common means of delivering courseware that is not offered online. For teachers and trainers, courseware content may include set-up information, a course plan, teaching notes, and exercises.

Courseware can include:

- Material for instructor-led classes
- Material for self-directed computer-based training (CBT)
- Websites that offer interactive tutorials
- Material that is coordinated with distance learning, such as live classes conducted over the Internet
- Videos for use individually or as part of classes

Tutorial

A tutorial is a Self-paced instructional program that provides step by step information in presenting a concept or learning unit. Computer based tutorials use interactive methods such as hyperlinks, and audio and visual presentation of the subject matter, and provide feedback through question-answer exercises. A tutorial is one method of transferring knowledge and may be used as a part of learning. More interactive and specific than a book or a lecture; a tutorial seeks to teach by example and supply the information to complete a certain task. Hence, a tutorial is the sub part of the class in which a teacher tries to solve the problems of the small groups of the pupils through individual teaching.

It is a self-paced learning exercise; a lesson prepared so that a student can learn at their own speed, at their convenience; Interactive class taught by a tutor to students at university or college, individually or in small groups; A tutorial is a class of between 5-30 students in which students discuss key topics, concepts and ideas with their tutors. Tutorials are closely linked to assessment and often involve small group discussions and group work. The tutorial typically is set up as a series of steps that progress through levels of difficulty and understanding. For this reason, the tutorial is best followed in its logical sequence in order to understand all of the elements of what the user is trying to learn.

A computer tutorial is an interactive software program created as a learning tool. Tutorials help people learn new skills by using a step-by-step process that ensures the user is following along and comprehending the material. For example, a Web development tutorial may begin with instructions on how to create a basic Web page. This page might only include the words "Welcome to my website" on it and use the minimum HTML required in order for the page to load in a Web browser. Once the user is able to create a working Web page, the tutorial may explain how to add other features, such as styled text, table layouts, and images, to the page. Then the tutorial may provide instructions on how to publish the Web page to the Internet. In British academic parlance, a tutorial is a small class of one, or only a few, students, in which the tutor (a professor or other academic staff member) gives individual attention to the students. The tutorial system at Oxford and Cambridge is fundamental to methods of teaching at those universities, but it is by no means peculiar to them (although it is rare for newer universities in the UK to have the resources to offer individual tuition). At Cambridge, a tutorial is known as supervision.

In some Canadian universities, such as York University or the University of Toronto, a tutorial refers to something more like an American discussion section, that is, a class of between 12-18 students that is supplemental to a large lecture course, which gives the students the opportunity to discuss the lectures and/or additional readings in smaller groups. These tutorials are often led by graduate students, normally known as a "Teaching Assistant" or "TA", though it is not unknown for the primary instructor of a course, even if a full professor, to take a tutorial.

Types of Tutorials

Tutorials are of three types :

Supervised Tutorials: In the supervised tutorials, the talented pupils and the teachers discuss the problems time to time. The pupils put up their difficulties. Then the teacher tries to solve those problems. In this way, after a discussion between a teacher and the pupils, the solution to some problems comes up.

Group Tutorials: Tutorials are conducted to solve the problems of the grown up pupils of average level. It should be remembered that the group tutorials can only be organized successfully by a teacher who possesses the full knowledge of Group Dynamics and Social Psychology.

Practical Tutorial: Practical tutorials are conducted to develop the physical skill and to achieve the objectives of psychomotor skill. Pupils have to work in the laboratory for this. Such tutorials are more useful for younger and pupils of lower classes.

Some people consider the teacher as primary and pupils as secondary in conducting the tutorials. In such a situation, if a tutorial acquires the form of a lecture, then this will be considered as autocratic strategy. Contrary to this, if the pupils are more active instead of the teacher, then it will definitely occupy its main place in democratic strategies.

Technical Report: Definition

Technical reports present facts and conclusions about your designs and other projects. Typically, a technical report includes research about technical concepts as well as graphical depictions of designs and data. A technical report also follows a strict organization. This way, when other engineers read what you write, they can quickly locate the information that interests them the most.

A technical report (also: scientific report) is a document that describes the process, progress, or results of technical or scientific research or the state of a technical or scientific research problem. It might also include recommendations and conclusions of the research. Unlike other scientific literature, such as scientific journals and the proceedings of some academic conferences, technical reports rarely undergo comprehensive independent peer review before publication. Where there is a review process, it is often limited to within the originating organization. Similarly, there are no formal publishing procedures for such reports, except where established locally.

General Format of Technical Report

Technical Reports have an organized format because a majority of your audience may not read the entire report in one reading. This specific format allows readers to quickly locate the information they need. Most technical reports include the parts listed below. However, you may be required to include or exclude specific sections. Be sure to check with your instructor before using the format outlined here.

- Transmittal Letter
- Title Page
- Abstract
- Report Body
- Introduction
- Method
- Results
- Discussion
- Executive Summary
- Table of Contents
- List of Figures & List of Apprevations
- References
- Appendices

The Thesis and Dissertation

Dissertation: An original study of a problem or a research investigation in complete or partial fulfillment of requirements for a higher degree of the university or other Institutions of Higher Education.

Thesis: A scholarly research report written to meet academic requirements, submitted by a scholar for a higher degree.

A dissertation or thesis is a document submitted in support of candidature for a degree or professional qualification presenting the author's research and findings. In some countries/universities, the word thesis or a cognate is used as part of a bachelor's or master's course, while dissertation is normally applied to a doctorate, whilst, in others, the reverse is true. The term dissertation can mean, more in general, a treatise on some subject, without relation to obtaining an academic degree. The term thesis can mean the central claim of an essay or similar work.

Thesis vs Dissertation – 8 Basic Differences

In some universities, dissertation and thesis are seen as the same thing, however, there are a number of differences between the two. Usually a thesis is submitted at the end of one's master's degree, and dissertation is submitted at the end of a Ph.D.

There are several differences between thesis and dissertation that one should know in order to clarify the concept of thesis vs dissertation. A thesis is basically the requirement for Master's degree while dissertation is the basic requirement to acquire the degree of doctorate. Let us review the 8 basic differences between thesis and dissertation in order to clarify our concept on thesis Vs dissertation:

- You have to utilize already collected information in order to prepare a thesis whereas dissertation is based on the research conducted all by yourself.
- Dissertation is lengthier, thus, takes more time to be completed while thesis is short; therefore, it does not consume too much time to be completed.
- In thesis, you may have to include a hypothesis based on your research work. In contrast to thesis, you should have a decent knowledge of the new discoveries in order to infer your conclusion effectively in dissertation.
- Thesis helps a student get scholarships while the case is indifferent in case of dissertation writing.
- In thesis, you have to focus on your primary argument in order to prove your standpoint to the readers. In contrast to thesis, dissertation focuses on your background work.
- In Master's thesis, you have to utilize the research work in order to prove your point; in case of PhD dissertation, you have to add novel findings to existing literature.

  Thesis is written as an academic research paper while dissertation is more like an academic book.
- Data collected in thesis is based upon the hypothetical analysis of contents whereas your dissertation is comprised of theory and argumentation based on original research.
- Thesis and dissertations follow the same outline as described for the research report. The major difference between the thesis and dissertation is length and comprehensiveness. Thesis or dissertation is to demonstrate the students' knowledge in a particular field, it is more appropriate to be complete and comprehensive rather than concise and brief.

Summarize the Difference

S.No.	*Thesis*	*Dissertation*
1.	It is submitted at the end of one's master's degree.	It is submitted at the end of a Ph.D.
2.	For a thesis, you have conduct original research.	For a dissertation you have to synthesize already existing literature.
3.	Thesis analysis is added to the already existing literature.	While dissertation is an analysis of the existing literature.

There were some of the most basic differences between thesis and dissertation. In some countries, thesis is done to obtain the doctorate degree and dissertation to acquire a master's degree; therefore, the difference between thesis and dissertation reverses in case of those countries. Although, thesis Vs dissertation is a debatable topic but many scholars would agree with the point that: "Thesis and Dissertation are the same, in general".

2.
Communication Skills

COMMUNICATION

Communication is a basic prerequisite of all human performance and interaction. In a broad sense communication refers to the transmission of thoughts, information and commands by employing the sensory channels. The art of communication ensures that the message is conveyed intact – undiminished and undistorted. Communication is also considered to be a process of exchange. i.e. give and take of information by message. Communication tries to blend into a mutual understanding of a fact, principle or theory.

Concept of Communication

The term 'communication' has been derived from the Greek word "Communis" which meaning 'to make common, or given and take mutual sharing.' Etymologically communication may be defined as:

(*a*) Sharing of ideas and feeling in a mood of mutuality.

(*b*) Involving interaction which encourages give and take.

(*c*) A process of sharing of experiences till it becomes common possession.

(*d*) A two-way process, including feedback and interaction.

According to Aristotle, communication is a means of persuasion to influence the other so that the desired effect is achieved. The Latin root of the word of 'communication' is 'communicare' which has three possible meanings:

(*i*) 'to make common' which is probably derived from either 2 or 3.

(*ii*) Cum + munus, i.e. having gifts to share in a mutual donation.

(*iii*) Cum + munire, i.e. building together a defense like the walls of a city.

Definition of Communication

- *James Carey,* defines communication as a symbolic process whereby reality is produced, maintained, repaired and transformed.
- *Dewey* defines communication as a process of sharing experience till it becomes a common possession. He says it modifies the disposition of both the parties who partake it.
- *Keith & Davis* defines it as a process of passing information and understanding from one person to another. It is essentially a bridge of meaning between the people. They opine that by using the bridge one can safely cross the river of misunderstanding.
- *Edger Dale* defines it as sharing of ideas, feelings in a mood of mutuality.

ELEMENTS / PROCESS OF COMMUNICATION / COMMUNICATION CYCLE

Communication is the process of linking between senders and receivers of the message. The communication process is made up of four key components. Those components include encoding, medium of transmission, decoding, and feedback. There are also two other factors in the process, and those two factors are present in the form of the sender and the receiver. The communication process begins with the sender and ends with the receiver. *Kumar, K.L* has listed the following elements of communications which are essential to understand communication models and network.

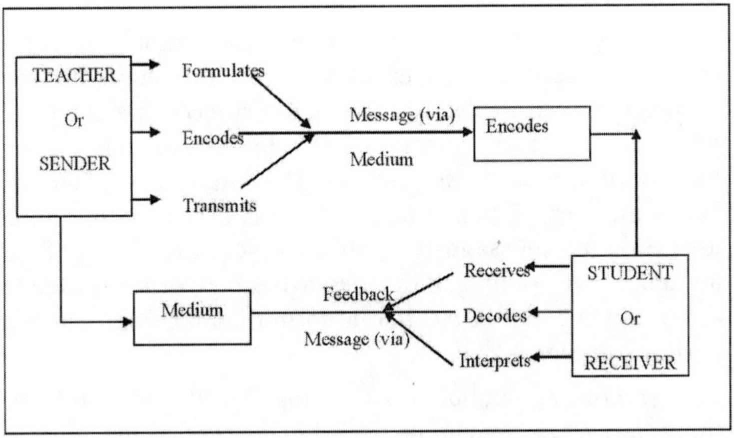

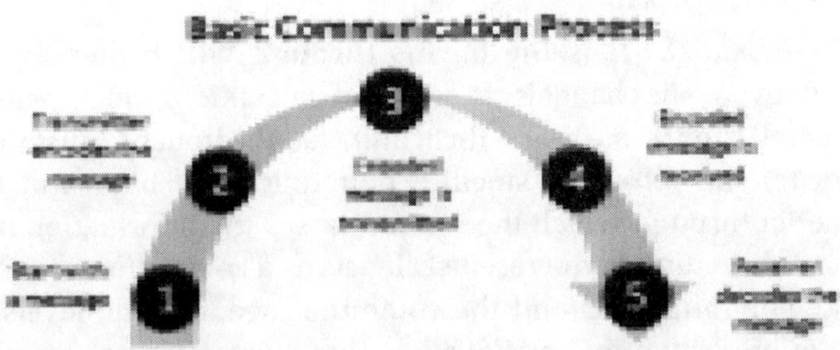

Sender : A person or an event which provides verbal or nonverbal cues to which someone can respond when the source is a person, he is called a sender (Teacher). The Source idea is the process by which one formulates an idea to communicate to another party. This process can be influenced by external stimuli such as books or radio, or it can come about internally by thinking about a particular subject. The source idea is the basis for the communication.

Receiver : A person who receives and interprets the message (student). The Receiver is the party receiving the communication. The party uses the channel to get the communication from the transmitter. A receiver can be a television set, a computer, or a piece of paper depending on the channel used for the communication

Message : A set of verbal or nonverbal symbols, gestures, cues, movements, figures or words sent by the source. Message, which is also known as the subject matter of this process, i.e., the content of the letter, speech, order, information, idea, or suggestion. The Message is what will be communicated to another party. It is based on the source idea, but the message is crafted to meet the needs of the audience. For example, if the message is between two friends, the message will take a different form than if communicating with a superior.

Symbol : A symbol is something that denotes an idea/ thing/fact etc. They can be verbal or nonverbal (eg. words - symbols-speech).

Channel : It is the means through which message is conveyed. The channels are senses of perception, which include visual (sight), auditory (hearing), tactile (touch), gustatory (taste) and olfactory (smell). Communication channel or the media through which the sender passes the information and understanding to the receiver. It acts as a connection between the communicator and the communicatee, i.e., the levels of communication or relationships that exist between different individuals or departments of an organization.

Encoding : It involves ciphering the message i.e., it is the process of using symbols to send the message. Encoding is how the message is transmitted to another party. The message is converted into a suitable form for transmission. The medium of transmission will determine the form of the communication. For example, the message will take a different form if the communication will be spoken or written.

Decoding : It involves deciphering of the message i.e., the process involves understanding and interpretation of the message sent. Decoding is the process where the message is interpreted for its content. It also means the receiver thinks about the message's content and internalizes the message. This step of the process is where the receiver compares the message to prior experiences or external stimuli.

Feedback : It is the response the receiver gives to the sender as a result of sender's message. Feedback, which is essential to make communication, a successful one. It is the effect, reply or reaction of the information transmitted to the communicatee. Feedback is the final step in the communications process. This step conveys to the transmitter that the message is understood by the receiver. The receiver formats an appropriate reply to the first communication based on the channel and sends it to the transmitter of the original message.

Noise : In any communication model, noise is interference with the decoding of messages sent over a channel by an encoder. There are many examples of noise:

Environmental Noise : Noise that physically disrupts communication, such as standing next to loud speakers at a party, or the noise from a construction site next to a classroom making it difficult to hear the voice of professor.

Physiological-Impairment Noise: Physical maladies that prevent effective communication, such as actual deafness or blindness preventing messages from being received as they were intended.

Semantic Noise: Different interpretations of the meanings of certain words. For example, the word "weed" can be interpreted as an undesirable plant in your yard, or as a euphemism for marijuana.

Syntactical Noise: Mistakes in grammar can disrupt communication, such as abrupt changes in verb tense during a sentence.

Organizational Noise: Poorly structured communication can prevent the receiver from accurate interpretation. For example, unclear and badly stated directions can make the receiver even more lost.

Cultural Noise: Stereotypical assumptions can cause misunderstandings, such as unintentionally offending Jews by wishing them a "Merry Christmas."

Psychological Noise: Certain attitudes can also make communication difficult. For instance, great anger or sadness may cause someone to lose focus on the present moment. Disorders such as Autism may also severely hamper effective communication

TYPES OF COMMUNICATION

(a) Non-verbal communication : Non-verbal communication is the process of communicating through sending and receiving wordless messages. Such messages can be communicated through gesture, body language or posture; facial expression and eye contact, object communication such as clothing, hairstyles or even architecture, or symbols and info graphics, as well as through an aggregate of the above, such as behavioral communication. Non-verbal communication plays a key role in every person's day to day life, from employment to romantic engagements.

Categories and Features of Non-verbal Communication

G.W. Porter divides non-verbal communication into four broad categories:

- *Physical:* This is the personal type of communication. It includes facial expressions, tone of voice, sense of touch, sense of smell, and body motions.
- *Aesthetic:* This is the type of communication that takes place through creative expressions: playing instrumental music, dancing, painting and sculpturing.
- *Signs:* This is the mechanical type of communication, which includes the use of signal flags, the 21-gun salute, horns, and sirens.
- *Symbolic:* This is the type of communication that makes use of religious, status, or ego-building symbols.

Static Features

- *Distance :* The distance one stands from another frequently conveys a non-verbal message. In some cultures it is a sign of attraction, while in others it may reflect status or the intensity of the exchange.
- *Orientation :* People may present themselves in various ways: face-to-face, side-to-side, or even back-to-back. For example, cooperating people are likely to sit side-by-side while competitors frequently face one another.
- *Posture :* Obviously one can be lying down, seated, or standing. These are not the elements of posture that convey messages. Are we slouched or erect? Are our legs crossed or our arms folded? Such postures convey a degree of formality and the degree of relaxation in the communication exchange.
- *Physical Contact :* Shaking hands, touching, holding, embracing, pushing, or patting on the back all convey messages. They reflect an element of intimacy or a feeling of (or lack of) attraction.

Dynamic Features

- *Facial Expressions :* A smile, frown, raised eyebrow, yawn, and sneer all convey information. Facial expressions continually change during interaction and are monitored constantly by the recipient. There is evidence that the meaning of these expressions may be similar across cultures.
- *Gestures :* One of the most frequently observed, but least understood, cues is a hand movement. Most people use hand movements regularly when talking. While some gestures (e.g., a clenched fist) have universal meanings, most of the others are individually learned and idiosyncratic.
- *Looking :* A major feature of social communication is eye contact. It can convey emotion, signal when to talk or finish, or aversion.

(b) Intrapersonal Communication : It is a communication transaction that takes place within the individual, this is the silent talking all of us do to ourselves such as thinking, remembering, dreaming and deciding. Intrapersonal communication is made possible because man become object to himself. That is he both produces and receives to same message. This type of communication fills more time in our experience because in every communication are always subject to our own private interpretation.

(c) Interpersonal Communication : It is the process of face-to-face interaction between sender and receiver such as group meetings, interviews, conversations among individuals. It has the advantage of a two-way communication with immediate feedback.

Characteristics of interpersonal communication:

- There is a perceptual engagement on the part of two or more people in physical proximity.
- Perceptual engagement allows focused interaction between a single focus of cognitive and visual attention as in a conversation. In focused interaction, each participant supplies cues supplies by other participant.
- In this focused interaction, there will be an exchange of messages. In this exchange, the participants represent to each other cues they think the other will interpret as intended.
- The interaction is face to face, therefore all senses may be utilized and participants confront each other totally.
- The interpersonal setting is unstructured; few rules govern form or content of interpersonal messages.

Interpersonal communication is very effective in influencing attitudes and behavior. Hazarded focused in its characteristics in that field:

- Personal contacts are casual, difficult to avoid.

- People are likely to put their trust in the judgment and view point of persons whom they know, like and respect.
- Personal communication influence people through what is said and by personal control in which the source is as important as the content itself.
- There is a great flexibility in the content of interpersonal communication. If the communication meets resistance from the receivers, he can change the line to meet their reaction.
- In face-to-face communication a person can ask questions, help direct the communication and make some control over it.
- In face-to-face situation, there is a chance for quick exchange of information. Two-way communication that gives a chance for immediate feedback to evaluate the effect of the signs one puts out, to correct to explain and to answer objections.
- In face-to-face communication it is possible to stimulate all the senses. It is also possible to communicate more for complete information.
- In face-to-face communication high percentage of the available information is non-verbal. The silent language of culture, gesture, body movement constitutes a large part of interpersonal communication.

(d) Group Communication : It involves a communication of a relatively larger group of people and lesser proximity among participants. It covers situations like a classroom, business meeting or attending a lecture/concert etc.

(e) Mass Communication : It is a process of creating shared meaning between mass media and their audiences. It involves a communicator using a mass medium to communicate with a very large audience.

Example :

(*a*) Telecommunications – communication over spatial distances using electronic means of communication,

(*b*) Radio and Television broadcasting etc.

(f) Spoken Communication : Oral communication is the sending and receiving of messages using spoken, verbal words, such as in interpersonal interactions or speeches. Examples of spoken communication that is used in the workplace include conversations, interviews, counseling/ helping colleagues, meetings, conferences.

Advantages of Spoken Communication

- Oral communication allows for immediate feedback such as the opportunity to ask questions when the meaning is not entirely clear.
- The sender is able to check and see whether if the instruction is clear or has created confusion.
- Spoken instructions are flexible and easily adaptable to many diverse situations.

Disadvantages

- Poor presentation of the message or the instruction can result in misunderstanding and wrong responses.
- Spoken communication is influenced by both verbal and non-verbal communication such as tone or body language which may skew the meaning of your message in the mind of the receiver.

(g) Written Communication : Written communication is the sending and receiving of messages through the written word, such as in e-mails, letters and text messages. Some of the main advantages and disadvantages of written communication are:

Advantages of Written Communication

- Written communication is good for complicated and vital instructions, which can be given in a precise and uniform manner.

- There is a lesser chance for the message to be misunderstood.
- Written instructions can be checked at a later date. It serves as a useful reference.
- Authority is transmitted more effectively with a written order than with an oral one

Disadvantages

- It is impersonal.
- People may not always read them.
- It does not answer questions and there is no immediate feedback.

BARRIERS TO COMMUNICATION

Barriers to communication can be classified into following categories. (Adapted from K.L. Kumar)

Physical Barriers	Environmental, Invisibility/Distance noise, Physical discomfort and ill health Distraction and improper time.
Language Barriers/ Linguistic Barriers	Verbalism, verbosity, language inadequacy, unclean graphics and symbols.
Psychological Barriers	Selective perception, disinterest, inattention, lack of motivation, poor concentration, redundancy, unrewarding experience, unfulfilled curiosity, anxiety, stress, emotions, prejudice, egoistic attitude, biased evaluation.
Background Barriers	Previous experiences, previous knowledge inadequate, cultural disparities, generation gap.
Organizational Barrier/Culture Barriers	Rules and regulations, hierarchical relationship, choice of media, lack of co-operation among communicators, indiscipline, group size.

1. Physical Barriers

(*i*) ***Environment:*** The overall environment of the place wherein the communication is taking place has an effect. The atmosphere, cordiality, temperature, etc., have a profound effect on communication.

(*ii*) ***Noise:*** The noise is any type of disturbance that interferes and reduces the clarity. Noise acts as destruction and withdrawal of attention. Noise is of four types:

- ***Physical Noise:*** The microphone tone being jarring or outside unrelated sounds.
- ***Psychological Noise:*** This refers to the individual's mindset which hampers his listening.
- ***Written Noise:*** Illegible, unsystematic writing leads to irritation and disinterest.
- ***Visual Noise:*** This refers to the time lag between sender and receiver.

(iii) Invisibility/Distance: A physical distance between sender and receiver especially in oral communication may lead to distortion of message. The loudness may not be sufficient to reach the person at a distance.

(iv) Physical Discomfort/Ill-health: If the seating arrangement is improper and chairs are of poor quality, the learner may be more conscious of it rather than concentrating on the message. Ill health may mar the senders and receiver's ability and capacity to communicate.

(v) Distraction: At times, the media selection may prove to be a distraction as attention is diverted. Also the outside influences may hamper communication process.

(vi) Improper Time: The best of communication done at an improper time may prove to be ineffective. For example, a teacher taking a class in games period or after school hours or during intervals may prove to be counterproductive

2. Language Barriers

(i) Verbosity and Verbalism: At times the language used by the communicator would be very high and bookish making it difficult to comprehend. Some communicators have the habit of talking uninterrupted, making the speech boring.

(ii) Language Inadequacy (i.e. Poor vocabulary and Grammar): Sometimes there might exist a language barrier since both sender and receiver do not comprehend each other's language. Also the sender may not be proficient in the language making his message unclear.

(iii) Unclear Graphics and Symbols: During written communication, if the sender uses some symbols which are not commonly used, then the receiver gets a wrong picture. Internationally there are some symbols and graphics. Any other when used may lead to improper understanding.

3. Psychological Barriers: In interpersonal communication the psychological factors like interest, attention, motivation, concentration of both sender and receiver have an impact. No one can be forced to perceive what he does not want to. It could lead to a situation wherein a person would be physically present but mentally absent. Negative attitudes and prejudices mar one's participation. Positive emotions of love, compassion and we feeling help in smooth flow of messages.

4. Background Barriers

(i) Previous Knowledge and Experiences: If the student has missed a link between past and present experiences/ communication, he would fail to appreciate the message. If past experiences have been dissatisfying and unrewarding the effect would spill over into the present communication.

(ii) Cultural Disparities and Generation Gap: If there is a cultural lag and generation gap between sender and receiver, it could lead to a distortion of message.

5. Organizational Barriers

(i) Rules and Regulations: Strict enforcement of rules, discipline may create an atmosphere wherein communication becomes formal and rigid.

(ii) Hierarchical Relationship and Lack of Co-operation: If there is a gap in the hierarchical positions, the communication would be affected.

(iii) Choice of Media: Some message may require personal communication and yet others may require use of audiovisual aids. Hence choice of media has a substantial influence on communication.

(iv) Group size: The type of communication to be used depends on the group size. A communication cannot think of the receivers as a "single mass". Each student is different from the other and the individual differences have an impact on communications.

SKILLS OF COMMUNICATION

Language learning is a skill. A language can be learnt by an individual not simply by knowing about the language; but by experiencing it. Playing football or cricket is a skill. One cannot become a good player of football by knowing all the rules and regulations if the game or by watching the game over a TV screen or mastering volumes of books on the subject. but one can learn the game by playing it physically and practicing it constantly. So is the case with learning a language. In the recent years, the emphasis has been shifted from the teaching of language as a system to the teaching of language as a means of communication. This has resulted in the teaching/ learning of a language as developing the four language skills, viz., listening, speaking, reading and writing.

Listening Skills

Listening is the fundamental skill of all the four skills and it is a major skill of learning in the teaching and learning process.

Meaning: To listen means to pay attention to paying attention to what is said, read, announced, spoken or played is listening. It is the beginning of the learning process. Without listening one cannot understand, learn or speak. According to Webster, to listen means to hear with attention. Horrworth breaks down listening into three different components which are hearing, listening and recognizing. Listening is accepted as one of the most effective modes of learning. In the words of Brown, "Listening ability lies at the very heart of all growth, from birth through the years of formal education". If the students acquire listening skill properly, they can easily learn the other skills of language learning.

Types of Listening

Listening may be classified into two categories, viz., Casual listening and focused listening.

Casual listening: Sometimes we listen to T.V. or radio commentaries or programmes while we are doing some work or talking with our friends. We can find majority of the audience is found busily talking among themselves rather than listening to what the speakers are blasting out through the microphones. This type of listening without any specific purpose is called 'casual listening'.

Focused listening: Sometimes we listen carefully, keenly and closely to find out the information we need to know. Listening seriously to the news bulletins on the radio or T.V. important announcements etc are a few examples of focused learning purpose. Oriented listening is focused listening. In this type of listening prior knowledge of the purpose of listening helps us to increase our concentration whenever we land upon some needed information.

Speaking Skills

Skill of listening and skill of speaking are interdependent and are the two sides of the same coin. i.e. Oral communication.

When the pupils have acquired a good number of words, it is time for them to acquire speech skills. We saw how language is primarily speech, and we also know that a good speech skill ensures good reading and correct writing.

Spoken English is important because

- Spelling offers no due to pronunciation
- Twenty six letters do the work of forty four sounds
- The same letter stands for different sounds.

- The same sound is represented by different letters.
- Silent letters do not work.

Reading Skills

Reading, of all the language skills opens up before us a new world of experience. We read for pleasure and profit and for information. There is vast literature, ancient and modern in English. We read newspapers, journals and magazines. In our day to day life we read reports, articles, notices, directions, timetables, maps and graphs to lead a purposeful life.

The learners benefit immensely if they are trained to read English through different stages of their education. The Kothari Commission recommended that English must be taught as a 'Library Language' i.e. mainly for reading purposes only. Reading is, perhaps the most useful skill that can be emphasized in teaching English language at secondary level.

Reading involves the process of recognition and conversion into appropriate sound value, reach of the bits of ideas separately and synthesis. Thus the meaning of the sentence is grasped. The two kinds of reading are oral reading and silent reading.

Oral Reading: words and sentences to be read are first drilled orally. Then pupils read from the blackboard after one or two model reading by their teacher. Then only pupils read from their text books. This is the procedure for all early reading lessons. Later, blackboard reading may be given up, but preliminary and preparatory oral drill will always be necessary. "Nothing to be read or spoken which is not already familiar to the pupils." All this apply to the detailed prose.

Silent Reading: It is introduced when pupils are able to recognize print words faster than they are able to pronounce them. In the beginning silent reading will be elementary like silently following another's oral reading, silently executing commands on blackboard or flash cards and answering questions on black board or flash cards after silently reading them. Then training in small paragraphs will be given. The unit gradually lengthens and full scale silent reading is began with the introduction of non-detailed texts and extensive readers.

Writing Skills

Writing is one of the expressive skills to be developed in a language. Before attempting to write anything, the student should be familiar with the reading of that work or structure and their meaning. When the child is able to recognize meaning, then he can ask to start writing. Writing provides reinforcement for reading and learning. It also provides a change of activity. Writing occupies an important place in school teaching as English is taught as a compulsory subject. Our students are examined not orally, but through writing. Writing helps us to record our thoughts and events accurately. 'Writing maketh an exact man said Bacon. So while teaching language we have to teach writing from the mechanics to a fairly advanced type of free composition.

The ability to write English implies mastering the mechanics of writing and using appropriate vocabulary and sentences with correct spelling and writing in a legible manner. Skill of writing is to be taken care of by the teacher as our students are expected to let us know their learning through writing only, especially at the time of tests and examination.

METHODS OF DEVELOPING FLUENCY IN ORAL AND WRITTEN COMMUNICATION

Oral Communication

Speaking is perhaps the most demanding skill for the teacher to teach. In their own language children are able to express emotions, communicate in tensions and reactions, explore the language and make fun of it, so they are expected to be able to do the same in any language. Most of the pupils have little opportunity to practice speaking language outside the classroom and so need lots of practice when they are in the class. There are lots of ways to improve oral fluency inside the classroom and in self interested activities. In the classroom oral fluency may be improved by practicing classroom second language, telling, stories, creating situations for dialogue, language, games and activities, use of language in social gathering, conducting interviews and telephone conversation. These activities of the classroom are done with the assistance of the language teachers.

Use dictionaries: For improving oral with fluency a good dictionary is so important. Sometimes students have to understand the meaning of the meaning too. The dictionary helps students to familiarize themselves with the language and also expose them to new words that they should find out the meaning. Students must us the dictionaries every time when they come across new word.

Sufficient Input: If students don't have sufficient input, the sentences they form will be wrong. If the sentences formed are wrong, and no one corrects them, they will start to think that what they have said is correct. Because of this their mind will be filled wrong sentences. Input is basically any correct language that you may hear or read. If you listen to an English radio station, that is input. If you read a book, then that is input. If you hear to fluent English speakers talking then that is input. If a fluent English speaker is talking to you in English then that is input. Reading the articles is input.

Reading Habit: Inculcate the habit of reading magazines which are available on a lot of different topic. No matter what subject interests you, there must be some magazines that talks about it. Find the magazines that interest you and read it cover to cover. Be sure to lookout for new words and new phrases and look them up in the dictionary as you go. If you cannot find a magazine of your choice, look for information you are interested in on the internet.

Listen to Radio and Television: The 'All India Radio' has some good programs that are designed to teach English to the listener. Besides this, there are also different radio stations available now a day in the big cities. Some of these radio stations are broadcasting matters in English. Listen to them to get a feel of the language. Listen to the news available on wide variety of TV channels. The news is a good place to get input of the language because it is spoken in a very clear, easy to understand way.

Chat with fluent speakers: Chat with fluent speakers real or online. Make friends with interesting speakers. Become pen-pals with a fluent speaker. While talking to them directly look at their movements of lips on how to pronounce words correctly.

Language learning software: Get a self learning language software and language learning kit.

Written Communication

Out of four skills of language learning, writing is a very important skill, as it serves as the medium through which we communicate our ideas, thoughts and feelings to other people who are at a distance from us. Language learning is incomplete without developing the skill of writing. Writing is needed to communicate to the other persons. It is used to make a record of events in specific fields. It is used to prepare documents, records, reports etc., with may be used as references in the future. Writing trains our mind through our senses particularly through eyes and ears.

Guidelines for Written Communications

The following guidelines and principles associated with effective written communication that you can refer to when creating and revising documents:

- *Clearly defined subject* : The subject or title of your material should be clear. The information contained in the material should satisfy the readers' needs.
- *Clarity* : Your message should be clear and easy for the reader to understand.
- *Conciseness* : Concise sentences are informative, brief and to the point.

- ***Credibility*** : The information should be accurate. Do your research before writing the material to make sure you can back up your claims or the information presented.
- ***Use words effectively*** : Use words the reader is more likely to understand.
- ***Use plain, simple words*** : Big words don't always convey the proper message.
- ***Be precise*** : Tell them what they need to know. Do not run on with useless words and language.
- ***Clarify technical language*** : Make sure the reader knows what you're talking about by using definitions when needed.
- ***Avoid over used words and phrases*** : It annoys people.
- ***Create readable sentences*** : Sentences should be understood without having to be read more than once.
- ***Write complete sentences*** : Try to use complete sentences whenever possible.
- ***Write efficient sentences*** : If the reader does not get the meaning of your message it's possible that your sentences were not as clear and helpful as they could be.
- ***Use an active voice*** - An active voice gets greater response from readers

Graded Exercises in Writing

Here are some exercises in writing, listed roughly in increasing order of difficulty.

- Pupils practice the correct strokes in writing the letters of the alphabet.
- Pupils copy single words from the blackboard, flash cards or from the text book.
- Pupils copy sentences from the text books and substitutions tables.

- Pupils re-arrange scrambled sentences.
- Pupils transform sentences; positive/negative, active/passive, declative/interrogative etc.
- Pupils match parts of sentences and write them out.
- Pupils fill in the blanks in a passages with appropriate prepositions, articles etc.
- Pupils described objects and pictures.
- Pupils write stories or describe events from a series of pictures.
- Pupils write letters to friends and relatives.
- Pupils write applications and business letters.
- Pupils write freely on a simple topic.

STYLE DICTION AND VOCABULARY

Diction

Diction (Latin: ***dictionem*** (nom. ***dictio***) "a saying, expression, word"), in its original, primary meaning, refers to the writer's or the speaker's distinctive vocabulary choices and style of expression in a poem or story. A secondary, common meaning of "diction" is more precisely expressed with the word enunciation—the art of speaking clearly so that each word is clearly heard and understood to its fullest complexity and extremity. This secondary sense concerns pronunciation and tone, rather than word choice and style.

"Diction will be effective only when the words you choose are appropriate for the audience and purpose, when they convey your message accurately and comfortably. The idea of comfort may seem out of place in connection with diction, but, in fact, words can sometimes cause the reader to feel uncomfortable. You've probably experienced such feelings yourself as a listener—hearing a speaker whose words for one reason or another strike you as inappropriate."

In a professional piece of writing, one of the most important decisions a writer must make is the type of diction he or she uses. Diction is the style of writing used based on word choice and usage. The type used is generally based on the appearance, sound, and meaning of the words the author wishes to use. Diction is important because it conveys the style of the piece - whether you want to write in a conversational manner or a direct, intelligent manner can be chosen by the types of words you use.

Types of Diction

The three main types of diction are slang, colloquial, and formal. Slang, or vernacular speech, is the "dumbed-down" version of writing, as most would say. It's used especially when you're trying to convey a sense of conversation or comfort ability in a piece of writing. The topic, in this case, would most likely be a softer, less-serious issue. The types of words used are ones that the average reader would easily be able to identify and understand, with large words and complicated sentences being left out.

Examples of slang diction would be: "He's game enough to play," "I finished my assignment just in the knick of time," and "He tried passing the buck after he was caught." Many idioms and euphemisms are often used in slang diction, to give it a fun feel. Informal language also falls into this category, which is language used in casual situations while still stating true facts.

The second type, colloquial language, is the "medium" type of diction. Generally, it uses a nice blend of slang and complicated words, as well as words that may take some background knowledge to understand. Regional dialect falls into this category, as do words people may be used to seeing but don't fully understand the meaning of. This is the most common type of diction, as it pertains to the every-day reader. Most newspaper and magazine articles are written like this.

The third type, formal or intelligent diction, is the smartest sounding, most complicated way to write something, It's mainly used in essay, especially ones centering around complicated topics. To the average reader, it involves looking up certain words and having trouble following the main points and ideas of the writing. Professors, scientists, historians, etc. use this type of diction when writing to fellow colleagues, and very little is this style of writing seen in every-day articles.

One of the main problems when choosing diction is accuracy. When choosing the proper diction, you must have a good and steady flow throughout the entire piece of writing. For example, you can't begin the essay with an educated, mature tone and then switch to slang half-way through. The reader may get confused, and the flow will become uneven. On the other hand, trying to connect to the reader with colloquial language while making valid arguments with large, complicated words will make the work sound sloppy.

Vocabulary

A vocabulary is defined as "all the words known and used by a particular person". However, the words known and used by a particular person do not constitute all the words a person is exposed to. By definition, a vocabulary includes the last two categories of this list

1. Never encountered the word.
2. Heard the word, but cannot define it.
3. Recognize the word due to context or tone of voice.
4. Able to use the word but cannot clearly explain it.
5. Fluent with the word – its use and definition.

Passive Vocabulary and Active Vocabulary

Even if we learn a word, it takes a lot of practice and context connections for us to learn it well. A rough grouping of words we understand when we hear them encompasses our "passive" vocabulary, whereas our "active" vocabulary is made up of words that come to our mind immediately when we have to use them in a sentence, as we speak. In this case, we often have to come up with a word in the timeframe of milliseconds, so one has to know it well, often in combinations with other words in phrases, where it is commonly used.

CLASSROOM COMMUNICATION AND DYNAMICS

Effective communication is the essential requirements for the success of teaching learning activities of any classroom. Therefore for all practical purposes, the teacher should invariably try for achieving utmost efficiency and effectiveness in the process of classroom communication and interaction with the students. For this purpose necessary improvement should be made with regard to the contribution of each factor and component related with the process and mechanism of classroom communication. Let us think about the role of these components on these lines.

*1. **Source of Communication:*** Effectiveness of classroom communication very much depends on the strengths and qualities of the sources of communication i.e. teacher. All teachers should therefore try to imbibe the virtues and qualities of an effective communicator or sender of the message. In brief the following things may contribute in improving the communicator image of a class teacher.

- Sound physical and mental health.
- Proper teacher like dress and mannerism.
- Proper teacher like behavior in dealing with the students.
- Appropriate voice, control and efficiency in the use of language mutually sharable with the students.
- Appropriate mastery over the subject matter, content or message delivered to the students.
- Proper knowledge, skill and efficiency in the use of various media and channels of communication.
- Efficiency in classroom control and response management.
- Efficiency with regard to thinking skills like ability to think and reason well, ability of imagining, creative

thinking, analyzing, synthesizing, generalizing or drawing inferences etc.

- Efficiency with regard to the use of audio-visual aids appliances and multimedia.
- Proper attitude towards self implying that the teacher as a communicator must possess self confidence in his abilities of believing, saying and doing.
- Proper attitude towards the students implying that the teacher should have a sense of respect, understanding and faith in the abilities of the students.

*2. **Communication Material:*** The effectiveness and success of the communication process in any classroom situation very much depends upon the quality and nature of the communication material. If the contents and message has some attraction, force and value to the receiver, it will surely catch his attention and make him quite attentive and active participant in the communication process. On the contrary, if there is nothing new, novel or valuable in the message or piece of instruction imparted by the teacher, it will neither attract nor motivate the students to take genuine interest for becoming active partner in the ongoing classroom communication. Therefore, it is the prime duty of the teachers to think seriously about the quality and nature of the content material and message given to their students.

*3. **Communication Media or Channel:*** Communication media or channels just lie in between the source and the receiver like a bridge or connecting link. What the teacher says or shows to his students can do it only with the help of some or the other verbal or non-verbal communication means. The nature and quality of the traffic flowing on the bridge is very much dependent on the appropriateness, strength and quality of the bridge. Similarly the effectiveness and strength of the communication flow between the teacher and students will surely depend upon the nature and quality of the verbal and non-verbal means, media and channels employed in the classroom communication. For this purpose the following things should always be kept in mind.

- Use that language which is quite known and under stable on the part of the students.
- The verbal means should be supported by the non-verbal clues, gestures, body language, physical movements etc. for giving required strength and effectiveness to the process of communication.
- To reduce the evil effects of verbalism, attempts should be made to make use of appropriate audio-visual aid material and appliances, suiting to the very nature and timing of the communication.
- Have variety, novelty and creativity in making use of different means and media for the communication of the intended message. Always prefer the multimedia approach over the single or the limited usual means.

4. Receiver of the Communication: Where the initiator or source of communication is the teacher, students lie on the other end for actualizing the process of communication. Actually what goes inside the classroom communication is always intended for the benefit of the students. That is why, it can only be carried out effectively with their active involvement and cooperation. In case the students are not interested or not capable of receiving and understanding the meaning of the message or do not respond in a proper way for maintaining the flow of communication, the communication, will turn into one side affair and thus lose its purpose and significance. These characteristics of the students for achieving required effectiveness in classroom communication may be summarized as below.

- They must have proper and sufficient previous knowledge and general background for receiving and understanding the communicated message.
- They must have required proficiency and abilities in terms of communication skills like listening, observing,

reading, writing, speaking, mapping, drawing, measuring, surveying, thinking, analyzing, synthesizing, evaluating and drawing inferences, etc.

- They must show proper zeal, enthusiasm, curiosity as well as need for maintaining the chain of communication.
- They must not put themselves into a passive recipient of the information or message given by the teacher but should make themselves, enquirer and active partner in the set up of the classroom communication.

*5. **The Environmental Conditions and Situations:*** The effectiveness of classroom communication also depends upon the appropriateness or inappropriateness of the situation or environmental conditions prevailing at the time of classroom communication. The psychological and physical factors involved in these environmental conditions and situations directly or indirectly influence the efficiency and effectiveness of the teacher (source), students (receivers) and media or channels of communication. Consequently efforts should be made for bringing necessary improvement in the environmental conditions and situations of the classroom communication by adopting the following measures.

- The classroom should be appropriately spacious as to accommodate the required number of students with the seating capacity norms. They should provide appropriate ventilation, lighting sound and seating arrangement along with sufficient space for instructional and communication activities.
- The classroom should be so situated as not to be affected by the outside disturbances, noise, etc.
- The classrooms should have all the necessary arrangement for the use of audio-visual material, equipment and appliances etc. needed for the effective classroom communication.

- As far as possible efforts should be made to have healthy and useful interaction between and among the teachers and students during the classroom communication.
- They should provide necessary encouragement as well as help in removing the communication difficulties and deficiencies by showing necessary sympathy and affection towards the students. Their responses should also be effectively managed and they should be provided with adequate remedial care and look after based on the feedback given by them in the process of communication.

In this way all round efforts are needed on the part of teachers for taking the students with them for the effective classroom interaction and communication by doing all what is needed on their part in terms of improving their own performances as communicator along with bringing necessary improvement in the mains, media and environmental conditions for drawing maximum advantage through the ongoing classroom interaction and communication.

Skills Required for Effective Communication

- Knowing what to communicate – It is very important for a sender to know what he or she intends to communicate to the receiver. Based on which the message needs to be framed and then transmitted to the receiver.
- Knowing the appropriate medium to communicate – Choosing appropriate means or mode of communication plays a very important role in helping the receiver understand or interpret as the message was intended while sent by the sender.
- Listening carefully and attentively - Listening to the message received carefully and attentively will give scope for better interpretation of the message sent and preparation for apt feedback to the message received.

- Not being judgemental – It is very important to receive the message without any judgement about the sender or about the message sent. On receiving the message or while sending the message being judgemental about the sender or the receiver by either of them would led to misinterpretation of the actual message.

3.

Communication Technology

Communication Technology

Electronic systems used for communication between individuals or groups. Communication technology facilitates communication between individuals or groups who are not physically present at the same location. Systems such as telephones, telex, fax, radio, television, and video are included, as well as more recent computer-based technologies, including electronic data interchange and e-mail. Communication technology is a term used to describe the various forms of correspondence that are available, including technological advancements. Communication technology includes new discoveries such as Internet communication, cell phones, etc Communication technology, also referred to as information and communication technology, is a term that describes all the technical means that process and communicates technology.

Developments of Communication Technology

The development of communication technology, technology which enables communication, has evolved over time. This evolution has had a significant historical impact; from the invention of the telegraph, which played a crucial role in the French Revolution, to the fire-fighters who came in on their days off after seeing the World Trade Center towers attacked on television in 2001.

1. Early Communications : Early forms of communication included runners, homing pigeons and smoke signals. The rise of communication technology came to make communication faster, more accessible and more efficient.

2. Printed Communication : Written communication thrived off of advancing technology, such as the invention of paper and the printing press. Ironically, continual advancement has lowered the need for printed publications, including newspapers and books.

3. Television : The concept of television developed from the idea of being able to see a person while interacting with her on the phone. As of 2009, the Federal Communications Commission (FCC) hopes that one day television will become an interactive form of electronic communication.

4. Internet : The Internet blossomed out of a 1967 study of Advanced Research Projects Agency (ARPANET) conducted by the United States Department of Defense. Internet-based electronic communication includes email, instant messages and social networking websites.

5. Wireless Communication : Radio technology is the basis of wireless communication. Wireless communication uses radio frequencies to function.

COMPUTER MEDIATED TEACHING

What is Multimedia?

Multimedia is media and content that uses a combination of different content forms. The term can be used as a noun (a medium with multiple content forms) or as an adjective describing a medium as having multiple content forms. The term is used in contrast to media which only use traditional forms of printed or hand-produced material. Multimedia includes a combination of text, audio, still images, animation, video, and interactivity content forms.

Multimedia is usually recorded and played, displayed or accessed by information content processing devices, such as computerized and electronic devices, but can also be part of a live performance. Multimedia (as an adjective) also describes electronic media devices used to score and experience multimedia content. Multimedia is distinguished from mixed media infinite art; by including audio, for example, it has a broader scope. The term "rich media" is synonymous for interactive multimedia.

Definition for Multimedia

"Multimedia means that computer information can be represented through audio, video, animation in addition to traditional media (i.e., text, graphics, drawing, images)".

"Multimedia is the field concerned with the computer controlled integration of text, graphics, drawings, still and moving images (video), animation, audio and any other media where every types of information can be represented, stored, transmitted and processed digitally". *–Readers Digest*

"The term multi-media approach to teaching-learning may be referred to the use of appropriate and carefully selected varieties of learning experiences which ,when presented to the learner through selected teaching strategies ,will reinforce and strengthen one another in such a way that the learner will achieve predetermined objectives in an effective way."

–Encyclopedia of Education

Multimedia means making appeal to different sense instead of one as in the traditional method. Multimedia includes high technology instructional media(HTIM) and low technology instructional media(LTIM). *–G.S.Pillai*

Characteristics of Multimedia

- Multimedia storage and retrieval systems contain more information than any human training agent can possibly embrace and have many terminals through which students have access to the information.

- The development of multimedia instructional and support systems have provided the tool for creating learning centers in which a very large number of models of learning can be actualized variation in complexity.
- By employing media technology as support systems we can offer to the students a large number of ways to learn a large number of things.
- What multimedia systems promise is a form which permits the delivery of a range or instructional and informational supports.
- Multimedia systems are not restricted to a single type of learning or instructional mode; they represent a support for a range of them.
- The capability of multimedia system is markedly greater than that of ordinary classroom practice, in creating a variety of learning models.

Criteria for Media Selection

Many media technologies are their own set of selection criteria. The factors for media selection are given under five groups. They are:

- Task factors
- Learner factors
- Physical attributes
- Instructional factors and
- Economic factors

Task Factors include:

- Objectives of the content
- Content variables
- Learning outcomes and
- Learner capability

Learner Factor includes:

- Group size
- Student interest
- Age
- Individual differences and
- Physical disabilities of the learner

Physical Attributes include:

- Visual Media
- Audio Media
- Motion and color Pictures and
- Real

Instructional Management Factors include:

- Instructional strategy
- Degree of teacher control
- Teaching learning styles
- Use of Media Taxonomies and
- Instructional Events

Economic Factors include:

- Cost Effective
- Availability
- Time
- Resources and
- Practicability

Categorization of Multimedia

Multimedia may be broadly divided into linear and non-linear categories. Linear active content progresses without any navigational control for the viewer such as a cinema presentation. Non-linear content offers user interactivity to control progress as used with a computer game or used in self-paced computer based training. Hypermedia is an example of non-linear content.

Multimedia presentations can be live or recorded. A recorded presentation may allow interactivity via a navigation system. A live multimedia presentation may allow interactivity via an interaction with the presenter or performer.

Elements of a Multimedia Programme

Elements in the Multimedia	*Method of Appearance*
Text	Information appears in the computer screen as sentences containing words.
Images/Pictures movies/Films	Photographs and diagrams appear movies could be run in the computer screen just like television programmes
Animation	Figures move and appear to be dynamic and alive (e.g. cartoons)
Audio	When a lion is presented and its roaring sound is also integrated with the visual
Interactive	Interactive multimedia programmes allow us to move in any direction laterally or linearly.we are able to interact with the programmes per our interest and expand our knowledge.

Image: An image (from Latin ***imago***) is an artifact, for example a two-dimensional picture, that has a similar appearance to some subject—usually a physical object or a person. Images may be two-dimensional, such as a photograph, screen display, and as well as a three-dimensional, such as a statue. They may be ***captured*** by optical devices—such as cameras, mirrors, lenses, telescopes, microscopes, etc. and natural objects and phenomena, such as the human eye or water surfaces. A ***moving image*** is typically a movie (film), or video, including digital video. It could also be an animated display such as a zoetrope.

Sound: Sound is a travelling wave which is an oscillation of pressure transmitted through a solid, liquid, or gas, composed of frequencies within the range of hearing and of a level sufficiently strong to be heard, or the sensation stimulated in organs of hearing by such vibrations.

Animation: Animation is the rapid display of a sequence of images of 2-D or 3-D artwork or model positions in order to create an illusion of movement. It is an optical illusion of motion due to the phenomenon of persistence of vision, and can be created and demonstrated in a number of ways. The most common method of presenting animation is as a motion picture or video program, although several other forms of presenting animation also exist.

2D animation: 2D animation figures are created and/or edited on the computer using 2D bitmap graphics or created and edited using 2D vector graphics. This includes automated computerized versions of traditional animation techniques such as of tweening, morphing, onion skinning and interpolated rotoscoping.

3D animation: 3D animation are digitally modeled and manipulated by an animator. In order to manipulate a mesh, it is given a digital skeletal structure that can be used to control the mesh. This process is called rigging. Various other techniques can be applied, such as mathematical functions (ex. gravity, particle simulations), simulated fur or hair, effects such as fire and water and the use of Motion capture to name but a few, these techniques fall under the category of 3d dynamics. Many 3D animations are very believable and are commonly used as Visual effects for recent movies. 2D animation techniques tend to focus on image manipulation while 3D techniques usually build virtual worlds in which characters and objects move and interact. 3D animation can create images that seem real to the viewer.

Interactivity : When we are viewing a frame containing a text or picture, in the multimedia programme, then to get further details regarding a fact (word) or figure (image) involved in the scene of the frame we have to press the hot spot over it by clicking the mouse and get at the related file.

Thus we are able to leap from a file to many related files of the programmed laterally also and get detailed knowledge about any concept, facts or figure.

Principles to Be Followed In Using Multimedia In The Classroom: (Matrix of learning)

While using multimedia in the classroom instruction, the instructor has to follow five basic principles.

Selection of Multimedia: It should be based on the learning objectives and characteristics of pupils. While selecting appropriate multimedia, the teacher has to consider the learner's cultural environment, past experience, physical and emotional make-up, needs, attitudes and visual literacy.

Readiness : The use of multimedia in the classroom instructions must be preceded by the learner's readiness for participating in the experience. The minds of the pupils must be prepared.

Setting the proper physical conditions : Physical facilities and conditions for using the multimedia must be as far as possible ideal so as to affect economy if time and to ensure active participation of the pupils. Proper seating arrangements, sufficient darkening facilities in the room and facilities for manipulating the different multimedia must be ensured.

Consolidation or follow up : Teachers should guide the learners in the response. For follow up work, suitable work sheet may be used.

Evaluation : Teachers should continuously evaluate the effectiveness of the multimedia and their techniques. The references points for assessment of the multimedia and methods are the specific learning objectives and performance criteria.

Approaches in Multimedia Learning:

Multimedia represents a potentially powerful learning technology, that is, a system for human learning. A practical goal of research on multimedia is to device design principles for multimedia presentation. In addressing the goals, it is useful to distinguish between the two approaches to multimedia design;

- Technology-centered approach and
- Learner –centered approach.

Technology Centered Approach: Technology –centered approach begins with the fictional capabilities of multimedia and these capabilities can be used in designing multimedia presentation. The focus is on how to incorporate multimedia into emerging communication technologies.

Learner Centered Approach: Learner centered approach offer an important alternative to technology-centered approaches. Learner–centered approaches begin with an understanding of how the human minds work and adopt multimedia to enhance human learning. The focus is on using multimedia technology as an aid to human cognition.

Multimedia Classroom Environment for the Learners

Learner–centered education is about a shift or change in educational design from existing traditional to the innovative practice for the betterment of education. Multimedia instructional network system based on information and communication technology is able to fulfill the learner needs and expectations, to attract learner's attention in the classroom, to involve them in a healthy learning environment. Multimedia instructional network based teaching and learning consists of learning content, network computer lab, software for teaching and learning. The multimedia classroom environments for the learners are as follows:

Hand Rising: If learners get doubts they can press the scroll lock key as a help button. The teacher hears a beep sound and gets a hand raise on a learners computer icon. Then the teacher can get into conversation mode with the learner and clear his doubts, while all the other learners overhear them. Instead of conversation, the teacher and the learner chat through remote messaging board also. The advantage in this case is there is more flexibility in getting the doubts cleared than the conventional class.

File Transfer and file submit: The teacher can transfer any file to any or all the learners to the desired location on the learner's machine. Through the file submit function the learner can also submit his work to the teacher electronically. File submitted by the learner gets stored in a particular location of the teacher machine which the teacher can go through anytime.

Net Movie: Through net movie video of MPEG and DAT format (VCD movie) can be played on the teacher machine and broadcasted to all the learners' screens in real time. It resembles as if the movie runs on the learners computers whereas, it is actually running on the teacher machine only, but the screen and the voice get transferred to the learner's machine. All this happens on just 100MBPS LAN network with no limitation on the number of learner machines. This is useful for showing a video content without the help of the projectors.

Group and group talk: The teacher can divide the learners into groups at will. One learner in the group is selected to work like the teacher and execute functions like Broadcast, audio broadcast, observe learner demo, intercom, file transfer and Net movie for that group. The selected learner and his computer act like the teacher and teacher-Machine for that group. The learners can be divided into multiple voice and message chatting groups. This is an excellent tool for group discussion.

Remote message: The teacher and the learners can communicate with each other by sending messages.

Small scroll: View the broadcasted screen in window mode with the teacher's mouse always in the centre.

One –to-one Voice chart: The teacher can talk with any one logged –in learner. The other learners always in the centre.

e-Content

e-Content means web-based instruction developed for individuals' auto learning on any subject required by the learners. The benefits of e-content for learners are including flexible schedule and instruction at convenient locations-homes schools and colleges. It informs learners about their progress and accomplishment. An important outcome of e-learning is e-Content. e-Learning is a process and e-content is a product. Many private institutions have come forward to prepare e-content materials for a limited number of subjects. At the higher education level, the University Grants Commission, New Delhi has allocated funds to those who are willing to develop e-Content on any subject. A few colleges have already started 'e-Content development cell'. At the school level, it is in the infancy stage. According to Information Technology policy, the Directorate of School Education, Government of Tamil Nadu has planned to introduce web-based instruction in the school from 2010-2011 onwards.

Difference between e-Learning and e-Content

e-Learning	*e-Content*
Objectives are general and not specified in behavioural terms	Objectives are specified in behavioural terms
Various ranges of technologies can be used for delivering the information	Any one of the technologies can be used to deliver instruction at a time
The duration of programme can not be fixed	The duration of programme can be fixed
Immediate feedback can not be collected	Immediate feedback can be collected
There will be no control over the situation	It is carried on under controlled situation
Pattern of interaction can not be studied objectivity	Pattern of interaction can be studied objectively.

Guideline for Creating Inputs for Development of e-Learning Module

For an effective and optimum development of both textual and visual e-learning module material certain guidelines need to be followed. The following components in the developed e-learning modules as given by the CEC-UGC.

- *Objectives:* In the development of e-learning module the first essential is a statement of objectives and description of the desired learning outcomes makes it clear to the users how the module will benefit them. The stated objectives enable then to organise their study effectively.
- *Modules:* Module refers to a configuration of sections, each having an independent theme leading to a coherent set of competencies. Beginning with the overview, each module contains a presentation of the content and self check exercise; Modules are independent structural experience containing objectives, learning activity and self check exercise. Each term is explained below:
- *An overview:* Overview represents a framework in which the contents of a module are presented. The content is divided into main sections and sub-sections. Each section presents at least one new point and generally each section related to a different objective of the module. The overview helps the learners to see what constitutes the module and thus to organise their study.
- *Content:* The content for presentation refers to the script about the topic. This may be equivalent to a narration of about 30-40 minutes duration. The audio-visual material related to the content is to be based on theories of instructional design. The following essential elements must be kept in mind when preparing text material for conversion into e-content.
- The criteria if relevance to the learners.
- The correctness of content
- The content should be broken into suitable small and relevant components rather than all to be dealt with at one stretch.

- The material should be arranged in a logical order keeping in view the following criteria : Moving from known to unknown, Moving from specific to general, Moving from simple to complex and Moving from basic to advance.
- *Assignment :* To check whether the learner has fully understood the material and can apply what has been learnt and/or, provide reinforcement to the learner, assignment type questions can be framed the questions set for assignment may be short answer type or essay type. The questions set must cover the entire unit and must emphasize on application, analysis, synthesis of the material by the learner.
- *References:* To tell the learners where the author found the specific information or where to look for more related information references must be sited. References consist of documents including journal articles, book chapters and unpublished work.
- *Glossary:* This refers and alphabetical list with meanings/explanation of the words or phrased used that may be difficult for learner to understand, for the e-content development. if considered necessary, glossary of the keywords used in the content may be developed.
- *Summary :* This expresses all the main points in the important task concepts, characteristic etc covered in the module IT enables the learners to check that the have completed all the necessary inputs. A summary may either be developed in the form of a simple outline of concepts featured etc. or be stated in the form of a list of key points covered.
- *Quiz:* This refers to a set of certain multiple-choice questions. Learners are given no time for preparation but are required to answer then and there. The answers can be checked with help of the computer so that the learner is provided immediate feedback.

- *Frequently asked questions (FAQ) :* Very often in the formal education system a teacher while planning a lesson envisages certain questions in advance and incorporates them in the course of his/her lecture. In the development of e-learning module these questions and their readymade answers are provided separately to the learners under what is now commonly known as FAQs. The purpose of these FAQs is to emphasis certain important aspects of the subject and to provide re-inforcement to the learner.
- *Discussion:* To increase comprehension to sustain interest through enhanced participation and to provide reinforcement, provision must be made for discussion for this purpose three or four broad areas related to the module may be outlined.
- *Feedback:* Feedback means seeking opinions regarding the material studied, to get the right kind of feedback a questionnaire comprising of related items may need to be designed.

SATELLITE-BASED COMMUNICATION

Educational Television (ETV)

Educational Television is a system that presents learning content in various subjects produced by an agency. It is a means of providing direct instruction (formal) as well as continuing education (non-formal). It has the capacity to bring the world into a classroom and a classroom into a home. India is a large country with varied climatic conditions, a large and ever growing population and vast tracts of inaccessible remote locations. T.V. as a mass medium has the potential to play a major role in the educational setup of our country.

Educational Television also refers to transmission of educational or information program or material by television. An instructional process that utilizes television program of and educational institution, it includes writing, programming and directing educational television programs.

Wayne Coy calls Educational Television as the "Electronic blackboard of the future" and lists the following as the characteristics of ETV.

- Educational Television combines both sensory and auditory experiences.
- It is an extension of the radio broadcasting.
- It offers uniformity of communication.
- It is versatile educational vehicle.
- It stimulates and reinforces ideas.
- It provides like broadcasts of "on the spot" events.
- It provides a powerful visual medium.
- It is a means for leisure time activities.

Historical Development of Educational Television

Television centered India four decades ago on September 15, 1959 (Audience Research Unit, 1991) as a pilot project founded by the Ford Foundation. It started with 20 TV receivers in and around Delhi, and transmitted one hour educational and developmental progammes twice a week. Over the years, the coverage of televison remained static. In other words, the emphasis was on consolidation rather than expansion. The coverage of Delhi transmitter and the duration of telecast, however, increased. Thirteen years later, the second television centre came into existence at Bombay on October 2, 1972. Between 1972 and 1975, four more ***Doordarshan Kendras*** (Television Centres) Srinagar (January 26, 1973), Calcutta (August 9, 1975), Madras (August 15, 1975) and Lucknow (November 27, 1975) were commissioned.

A significant landmark in the history of television in India was one year Satellite Instructional Television Experiment (SITE) launched on August 1, 1975 involving 2330 villages of the economically back ward states.

The following educational television projects have been introduced in India:

1. Secondary School Television Project,
2. Delhi Agriculture Television (DATA) Project (Krishi Darshan),
3. Satellite Instructional Television Experiment (SITE),
4. Post - SITE project,
5. Indian National Satellite (INSAT), and
6. Higher educational television project (HETV) of UGC.
7. Country wide classroom TV project (CLASS)

Role of Educational Television

1. Improvement of quality.
2. Television as a means of extending children's experience.
3. Television as means of introducing affective education.
4. Television as a means of equalising educational opportunity.
5. Television as a means of improving efficiency and productivity.
6. Television - based instructional systems.

Limitations of Educational Television

1. It is a one way communication
2. Problem of pacing learning
3. Low and poor accessibility
4. Costly affair both production and receiving
5. Difficult to integrate T.V. and classroom teaching.
6. Visuals become a source of distraction.

Role of Teacher in Educational Television (ETV)

The five stages in ETV in which a teacher needs to be involved are :

(a) ***Planning and preparation of Programme***: The ultimate user of the ETV programme is the teacher, hence the teachers role in making decisions regarding the content, matter and sequence is of utmost importance.

(b) ***Production of programme***: The production of an ETV programme involves a lot of technical knowledge, but the knowledge of the mechanics of production helps him in contributing to the editing and modification stages.

(c) ***Presentation of Programme***: TV presentation requires some extra skills other than classroom teaching skills. So a teacher should be competent to present a lesson in the studio.

(d) ***Utilization of Programme***: The teacher should be able to lead the follow up programme after viewing ends. The teacher has to get the pupils ready to watch a program by providing necessary background information and later on conclude based on observations after viewing of the program. He should be in a position to clarify doubts and elaborate certain missing links.

(e) ***Evaluation of the Programme***: The teacher should be trained to evaluate all aspects of the program so that he will be in a position to suggest modifications both in content and style of presentation.

Educational Radio

Radio has been playing an important role for promoting relevant and interesting education. It brings the outside world into classrooms and makes educational programme very attractive and useful. It not only informs, but also inspires the audience. It inculcates values, develops virtues and encourages imagination. Therefore, radio has been used as a potential medium for helping in realization of educational objectives most efficiently. Being an inexpensive medium, it has reached villages and is now available in the nook and corner of the society. Radio is, at present, not only one of popular mass media, but also a potential instructional tool in the formal, informal and non-formal education.

Radio broadcasts started in India in 1927 with two privately owned transmitters at Bombay and Calcutta. The government of India took them over in 1930 and started Indian Broadcasting Service. In 1936, this name was changed to All India Radio (AIR). Since 1957 it is known as *Akashvani.* It has been made a separate department. Air is now the biggest media organization of the Ministry of Information and Broadcasting. Its programmes are received by over two crore-radio receiver sets in India. It is serving as an effective medium to inform and educate people and to provide healthy entertainment. It is also helping in creating a climate of opinion in which social change can take place and people could be involved in the process.

In 1947, All India Radio's network consisted of six radio stations. Now there are more than one hundred stations covering all the important cultural and linguistic regions of the country. The programmmes are radiated from 264 transmitters covering 95 percent of the population spread over 78.33 percent area of the country.

Characteristics of Educational Radio

- Easy Accessibility.
- Wide Coverage.
- Low Capital Investment and Operating Costs.
- Easy Production.
- Feasible Mode of Learner Enrichment.
- Effective Means of Thought Promotion.
- Effective Recreation/Transmission of Reality.
- Cheap Mode of Thought Promotion.
- Supporter of Motivation for Learner.

Educational Implications of the Radio

Radio has a distinctive role to play due to following reasons:

(*a*) Radio extends the area of acquaintance

(*b*) It brings people of rare contribution to the learners

(*c*) It placers events of current nature at the hands of the listener

(*d*) It helps in inculcating values

(*e*) It helps slow learners and pupils having poor sight

(*f*) It can be used as a medium to teach all subjects particularly language and music

(*g*) It refreshes Knowledge of teachers

(*h*) Wide Coverage

(*i*) Cheap Medium

(*j*) Easy repair and low maintenance

Limitations of Radio Broadcasting

- It is not a flexible medium – No face to face interaction. It is a one way communication process.
- Provisions for feedback are time consuming.
- It cannot be used effectively for all subjects especially sciences.
- Production of radio programmes requires expertise. It is only an auditory presentation and very little of what we hear, we can remember.

Satellite Communication and Satellite Instructional TV Experiment (SITE)

When Abraham Lincoln was assassinated in 1865, the news took 12 days to reach Europe. About 100 years later, when john F. Kennedy was assassinated, the world knew it immediately. The news travelled to the farthest corners of the world at the speed of light. Today television viewers the world over are able to see every big event that is happening in any part of the globe simultaneously with the help of communication satellites.

The micro electromagnetic waves (MHz or GHz range) travel in straight lines, and these are used for television transmission. Only line - of - sight communication is possible with this type of transmission. The range of terrestrial TV stations is limited to within 100 km in line-of - sight. This can be increased slightly by raising the height of the tower or by introducing microwave repeater stations. As an alternative, a geostationary satellite at a height of 35, 650 km in effect the visual horizon.

The satellite revolves in a circular orbit at an altitude of 35, 650 km where it takes 24 hours to make a complete revolution and this coincides exactly with the period of rotation of the earth about its axis. If the direction of travel of such a satellite is the same as that of earth's rotation, and if its orbit lies in the earth's equatorial plane, the satellite moves synchronous with the earth and thus appears to be geo-stationary.

The television programmes were related to education, agriculture, health, family planning and national integration. Telecasting was made for four hours a day out of which one and half hours in the morning were meant for primary school children and two and half hours for adults in the evening. The project was intended to cater to the needs of people in rural community. This Satellite Instructional Television Experiment (SITE) of 1975-76 was the first milestone for TV transmission in India.

The first Indian experimental geostationary satellite APPLE (Arisane Passenger Payload Experiment) was followed by INSAT - IA which unfortunately died a premature death. Subsequently the INSAT-IB was launched and ETV programmes were telecast on 30 August, 1983. The new multipurpose satellite, INSAT-IB was expected to give a fillip to the expansion of TV network in our country. Two transponders were an available for TV telecasting and it was intended to extend TV service to remote backward areas in six states-Andhra Pradesh, Orissa, Maharashtra, Bihar, Gujrat and U.P. Programmes were telecast in the afternoon for colleges and university students as well as special programmes in the evening for women and children. INSAT-IC was put into operation after its launching on 22 July, 1988. The multipurpose satellite, INSAT-ID was put into orbit successfully and has proved the ingenuity and ability of the Indian scientists and technologies. With the help of INSAT now, it is possible to develop to national and regional network of TV service of high quality and good international standard.

Software centers for preparation of instructional materials were located a Jamia Millia (New Delhi), Central Institute of English and Foreign Languages Studies (Hyderabad) and at university centers at Pune, Gujarat, Osmania and Roorkie. The programmes are not about individual lessons but are concerned with enriching the students' Knowledge. According to the Ministry of Information and Broadcasting the major educational objectives of a satellite television would be to promote alternative approaches to education for children, youth and adults. The thrust of the specific programmes would be to emphasize direct teaching, moving away from curriculum - oriented approach and aim at reduction of load in the classroom.

Growth of Indian Satellite

Year	*Satellite*	*Year*	*Satellite*
1975	ARYABHATA (First Satellite)	2000	INSAT – 3B
1979	BHASKARA – 1	2002	INSAT – 3C
1980	ROHINI	2002	KALPANA – 1
1981	APPLE	2003	GSLV – D2
1981	BHASKARA – II	2003	INSAT – 3A
1982	INSAT -1A	2003	INSAT – 3E

Year	Satellite	Year	Satellite
1983	INSAT -1B	2004	EDUSAT
1987	ASLV	2005	CARTOSAT, HAMSAT
1988	INSAT – 1C	2005	INSAT – 4A
1990	INSAT – 1D	2006	INSAT – 4C
1992	INSAT – 2A	2007	INSAT -4CR
1993	INSAT – 2B	2008	CHANDRAYAN-I
1995	INSAT – 2C	2010	BRAHMOS
1999	INSAT – 2E	2011	PSLV-C17

The Objectives of SITE Programme

(*i*) To show the potential value of SITE in the rapid development of effective mass communication.

(*ii*) To ascertain the workability of Satellite-based instructional television system in our rural areas.

(*iii*) To demonstrate the potential value of Satellite broadcast television programme in the practical instruction to the children and adults of rural village.

(*iv*) To stimulate national development in our country with important economic technological and social development.

Areas of SITE

(*a*) Technology – learning situation, instructional and educational programme.

(*b*) Service Teacher Training Course

(*c*) Programme on Agriculture.

(*d*) Health and Family Planning.

(*e*) Adult Education and Non-Formal Education mainly distant education.

THE EDUSAT (Educational Satellite)

EDUSAT is the first Indian satellite built exclusively for serving the educational sector and was launched successfully by GSLV-F01 on 20-9-2004. It is mainly intended to meet the demand for an interactive satellite based distance education system for the country. It strongly reflects India's commitment to use space technology for national development, especially for the development of the population in remote and rural locations.

The 1950 kg EDUSAT was launched from Satish Dhawan Space Centre (SDSC) SHAR, Sriharikota, into a Geosynchronous Transfer Orbit (GTO) by ISRO's Geosynchronous Satellite Launch Vehicle (GSLV). EDUSAT was placed in the 36,000 km high geostationary orbit and co-located with INSAT-3C and KALPANA-1 at 74° East longitude.

Operator	ISRO
Major contractors	ISRO Satellite Center, Space Applications Centre
Mission type	Communication satellite
Satellite of	Earth
Orbital insertion date	2002-09-24
Launch date	2004-09-20 at 10:31:00
Launch vehicle	GSLV
Carrier rocket	GSLV F01
Launch site	Satish Dhawan Space Centre - First launch Pad

Mass	1,950 kg
Power	2040 Watts Solar Panels
Batteries	24 AhNi-Mh
Regime	Geo Synchronous Orbit
Eccentricity	0.0
Inclination	0°
Altitute	36000 km
Orbital period	24 hours
Longitude	74°E
Orbits per day	1

Satellites can establish the connectivity between urban educational institutions with adequate infrastructure imparting quality education and the large number of rural and semi-urban educational institutions that lack the necessary infrastructure. Besides supporting formal education, satellite systems can facilitate dissemination of knowledge to the rural and remote population about important aspects of health, hygiene and personality development and allow professionals to update their knowledge base as well. Thus in spite of limited number of trained and skilled teachers, the aspirations of the growing student population can be met through the concept of tele-education. The concept of beaming educational programmes through satellite was effectively demonstrated for the first time in India in 1975–76 through the Satellite Instructional Television Experiment (SITE) conducted using the American Application Technology Satellite (ATS-6). During this unique experiment, which is hailed as the largest sociological experiment conducted anywhere in the world, programmes pertaining to health, hygiene and family planning were telecast directly to about 2400 Indian villages spread over six states. Later with the commissioning of INSAT system in 1983, a variety of educational programmes had been telecasted.

The major advantages of satellite-based Distance Education include:

- Simultaneous delivery of lecture sessions to a large number of geographically dispersed people in the shortest time
- Uniformity of the lecture content
- Access to the subject expert and his/her lecture material
- Repeatability of delivery of lectures from the archives
- Capability to share the same network by different user groups
- Significant savings in expenditure due to economies in travel, logistics and
- replication of teaching infrastructure

The scope of EDUSAT Project will be realized in three phases:

- Phase-I: This is the pilot phase of the overall project that will be implemented in three states – Karnataka, Maharashtra and Madhya Pradesh – using INSAT 3A in Ku-band. Visvesvaraya Technological University (VTU) is one of the beneficiaries of this project in Karnataka
- Phase-II: This is the semi-operational phase that uses new technology, DVB-RCS (Digital Video Broadcast-Return Channel through Satellite). The network will be expanded to cover two more states and a national institution through EDUSAT.
- Phase-III: In this phase, the entire country will be covered using six regional beams and one national beam by enlarging the network and making it operational.

Broadcast Content

- Regular School/College curriculum (started)
- Coaching for AIEEE (started)
- Training on Soft Skills (under development)

Objectives of EDUSAT

- Providing uniform, good quality of curriculum teaching for final year students of colleges.
- Senior Secondary Schools and primary schools, and also for technical institutions.
- Improving the level of science education among the students, as well as to improve English.
- To ensure that teacher absenteeism does not disturb the study of children.
- Reviving the interest of children in classroom studies.
- Providing quality teacher training, so as to improve the subject knowledge of the teachers.
- As well as to train them to use ICT in education.
- To improve the 'soft skills' of the students, so that they are able to obtain employment.
- To train children for appearing for All India Professional Course Entrance Examination.
- To train/familiarize them about appearing in examinations with 'objective type' questions.
- To provide access to quality education, particularly for far flung/remote location schools.

Positive Outcomes/Changes from the EDUSAT Project

- The most significant out come from the project is that for the final year science students in Government Senior Secondary Schools, the full syllabus is being covered through uniform good quality subject teaching. Similarly, for the final year students of colleges, the majority of the course content of Science, Commerce & English and the difficult topics of some other important subjects, is being fully covered through uniform quality teaching.
- While Government has approved filling up of vacant posts through guest faculty, it is ensured through use

of EDUSAT that even where a teacher is absent, uniform quality instruction is provided to the children.

- The project has led to a significant enhancement in the interest of the students for the science stream. A large number of demands have been received to start science stream in Government schools and colleges next year.
- The project has led to a much greater interest amongst students in class room studies. In addition to the live lectures, the resource persons are using multimedia, including slides and video clippings.
- For recorded lectures, 'animations' are also being used, so that there is not only greater interest among the students, but also enhanced conceptual clarity of the subject.
- There is exceptional enthusiasm among the teachers, who have been selected as the resource persons. There is also great interest among the teachers for obtaining training on use of ICT in education.
- The programme for improving soft skills of children will, at the school level, improve the basic English language skills, and at the college level, it will definitely improve employability of the graduating students, since, in the Soft skills programme there is the added innovation that a graduating student who clears the end of course exam securing more than 50% marks, will be ensured employment by the private collaborating agency.

COMMUNICATION THROUGH WEB

Internet

Internet is the world's largest computer network, the network of networks, scattered all over the world. It was created nearly twenty-five years ago as a project for the U.S

Department of Defense. ***Richard Kleinrock*** is considered the ***Father of Internet*** and *TCP/IP* is considered as the ***Mother of Internet.***

The Internet is a global network of computers that allows many million of computer users to share and exchange informations. Internet is a rich source of informations. Many thousands of computers are linked to the Internet, hold vast quantities of data that you can access from your personal computers whenever you want. Teachers, students, businessmen, doctors, engineers, scientist etc. can get recent data from internet which makes their knowledge up-to-date. Accessing the informations through internet is much faster. Informations can be downloaded into the computer and print out can be taken.

Origin and Development of Internet

1957	ARPA was formed
1969	ARPANET was commissioned for research into computer networking.
1971	E- mail and e-mail utility became available
1973	First international connections to ARPANET. University College of London and Royal Radar Establishment, Norway.
1974	Telnet
1975	Operational management of the internet transferred to DCA (DISA).
1979	USENET; ARPA established the internet Configuration Control Board (ICCB).
1982	TCP/IP suite declared as standard of Department of Defense.
1983	MILNET separated from ARPANET.
1984	Domain Name System introduced; number of hosts exceeds 1000.
1985	Domain name registration system introduced

1986	NSFNET was established; IETF and IRTF came into existence under the IAB.
1988	Internet Relay Chat developed.
1989	Number of hosts exceeds 100,000.
1990	ARPANET ceases to exist; Dial up internet connections by ILSPs
1991	WAIS, Gopher and World Wide Web.
1992	Internet Society is chartered; Number of hosts breaks 1,000,000 Veronica released.
1993	Business and media take note of the internet; Mosaic takes the internet by storm.
1994	ARPANET /internet celebrates 25th anniversary; shopping malls on the internet.
1995	NEFNET reverts back to research network Main US back bone traffic re-routed through interconnected network providers. Search engines developed.
1996	Government restrictions on the internet use around world.

World Wide Web

Many people believe that both internet and World Wide Web are same. But actually it is not the true. WWW is a type of service in the internet. i.e., Internet is the backbone of communication systems whereas WWW is a type of service that uses communication systems.

A Web is a collection of Web sites and the Internet is a network of networks. WWW is nothing but the collection of Web sites on the Internet and the sites are all linked together somewhat like the strands of a spider Web. The World Wide Web is often abbreviated as the Web or WWW of W3.

WWW was created in 1989 by the Tim Berneis Lee at the European laboratory for particle physics (CERN) in GENEVA, Switzerland to enable the document communication between the physics researches and to create a network between them, physics researches created hypertext documents as their documentation standards.

The WWW contains huge amount of information which a user can access using a browser such as Internet explorer or Netscape Navigator. The documents accessed are in the form of web pages. Web pages may contain text, graphics, icons animation, sounds and video-multimedia capabilities and are usually user-friendly.

1. ***Website:*** A Web site is a collection of interconnected Web pages. Usually there is a main or home page which provides link to the other pages and vice versa. Each page (document) has its unique URL.
2. ***Web Language:*** HTML (Hyper Text Markup Language) has become as the standard Markup Language or information publishing.
3. ***Web pages:*** A webpage is a HTML document that is stored in a web server and that has an URL so that it can be accessed via the web. It is a single unit of information often called a document. It consists of text, images, background and colour effects, links, java applets, vbscripts etc.,

   For Example: www.bdu.ac.in is the website name and it consists of several web pages like index.html, syllabus.html, course.html, result.html etc.,
4. ***Home Page:*** A home page is the front door of the web site. When the web user is typing a website name in the browser, the homepage will be displayed first. For Example: www.yahoo.com takes you to www.yahoo.com\index.html.
5. ***Web Browsers:*** A Web Browser is a software tool that computers use to communicate with web servers on the internet. Web browsers enable to download and display the web pages that user requests.

A Web Browser should be capable of understate HTML and display text. Now Web Browser supports pictures, video, sound and even 3D images. In the address bar of the browser, type the URL and it will display the web pages. The famous browsers available are

(a) ***Microsoft Internet Explorer (IE)***: This browser is shipped freely with almost all products of Microsoft and is tightly coupled with the operating system. It comes with outlook express, an e-mail client for downloading the e-mail messages from the server to the local machine.

(b) ***Netscape Navigator:*** Netscape offers a close competition to Microsoft and it offers a better support to display java applets than IE. Netscape also offers the email client besides other functionalities like HTML editor and calendar.

(c) ***Others:*** Opera, Konqueror and Mosaic are some of the other popular browsers in the market.

Differences between Internet and Web

Internet	Web
1. It is the network of networks.	It is the network of websites.
2. It is considered to be a carrier.	It is going to travel on it.
3. It is Hardware Approach.	It is Software Approach.

Applications of Internet

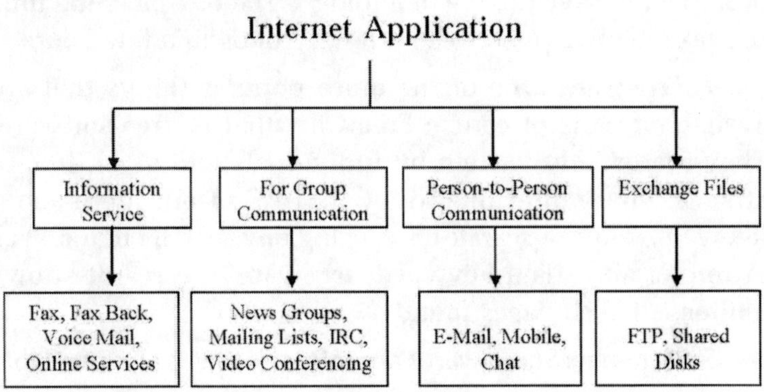

General Applications of Internet in Education

1. ***Video conferencing:*** Video conferencing allows face-to-face conversations with other people on a network. Whether they are living in the city or far away. Using videoconferencing software & equipment, you can see and hear the people you are communicating with. Videoconferencing allows the exchange not just of voice and graphics but also of moving images. Videoconferencing technology does not use telephone lines but either a satellite link or television network (broadcast/cable). Web-based conferencing, as the name implies, involves the transmission of text, and graphic, audio and visual media via the Internet; it requires the use of a computer with a browser and communication can be both synchronous and asynchronous.

2. ***Electronic Mail (E-Mail):*** E-mail is the widely used communication service between Internet users. E-mail transmits the message between any two computers. Users login to their mail-id and send emails to anyone. E-mail not only contains the message alone but also images, sound and video. It is possible to attach all types of files in the e-mail. The signatures can also be attached at the end of the e-mails.

3. ***Down loading:*** Many websites offers files for download (free or otherwise) when you click on a link to download file, the file Download dialog window will open. You are prompted to save the file in a folder. The downloading time can take anywhere between a few seconds to a few hours.

4. ***Free ware:*** One of the more popular things that are available free is of course Freeware, that is, free software. They are usually written by individuals and given free to anyone who would like to try it. To find out more about freeware, you can search for it using any search engine. For example: alta Vista-keyword 'freeware'-the result shows millions of Web pages found.

5. ***Shareware:*** Share wares are software that is also available for download from the Internet but they are not free.

However you can download an evaluation copy of a program to tryout for certain number of days. The evaluation copies usually do not contain all the features of the complete program. If you like the program, then you can purchase the complete one by ordering it through the Internet. Some shareware programs come complete and the authors usually request that you, the user, pay for the programs if you want to continue using them after the trial period.

For Example: Alta Vista- keyword 'shareware'-the result shows millions of Web pages found.

6. Tel net: The process of remote login (correcting to a Computer located in the next room, the next town on in another country) is established by a set of rules that endless one computer to correct to another computer. Telnet allows the user to access internet resources is available through telnet. Example: Library catalogs database, Grapier, www.

7. News Group: News Group (Usenet) is a worldwide discussion medium. It is also referred to as network News or Net news. Millions of users read Usenet articles daily and post their Views. It is more like a huge bulletin board service with hundreds of message areas on news groups. The news groups in the Usenet are organized hierarchically with categories, groups and subgroups. For example: The 'sci' category includes several subgroups such as mathematics and physics. The mathematics subgroup again has a number of subgroups.

Example of Usenet News Groups

alt. bbs Internet	-	Link of internet.
soc culture Indian	-	culture of India
sci-space news	-	NASA and other space News .

8. Internet Relay chat (IRC) (chat): IRC is a facility for fascinating discussion. It is basically a chat program that allows several users spread all over the globe to chat simultaneously. This is a real time connection and the users' and receive typed message as they are entered on the keyboard.

Chat is an acronym for Conversationally Hypertext Access Technology by which any message can be simultaneously sent to any user in any corner of the world. By this a live conversation is possible. With the minimum cost the message can be transferred.

9. Blog: An individual can make an individual websites. And then an individual can note his thought experience in the websites. It is a short for web log. This is a web-based publication where you can regularly add text, photos, audio files, and/or links, and is often likened to a diary. Authoring a blog, maintaining a blog, or adding an article to an existing blog is called 'blogging'. Blogs can be published by groups or individuals, for a variety of purposes. These are great for students to keep a record of the development of projects, research information links, and to reflect on their learning.

10. E-Learning: An innovative application of computer in the teaching and learning process is e-learning. E-learning may be network-based, intranet-based or internet based, which includes text, video, audio, animation and virtual environments. E learning provides faster learning at reduced costs, increased access to learning, and clear accountability for all participants in the learning process.

11. E-Journals: The journals which are web based and available online are known as e-journals. These e-journals have been considered to be one of the significant applications of computer in the field of education. Journals tend to come from two sources. Commercial publishers and titles published by associations and societies. There are varieties of access levels, title availability and pricing mechanisms.

12. Virtual University: The term "virtual university'" characterizes an organization that provides higher education on the Internet. Some of these organizations are truly "virtual", existing only as loosely tied combines of universities, institutes or departments that provide together a number of courses over the Internet. Others are real organizations with a legal framework, yet named virtual because they appear only on the Internet.

In future, an international library many be a small room with Internet facility; a Virtual University may be something like a small house and the classroom may be their monitor. This is possible, as the Internet technology is growing with an unbelievable speed.

INTERPERSONAL COMMUNICATION THROUGH WEB

The following are the interpersonal communication through web:

Blogs: The term web-log, or blog, was coined by Jorn Barger in 1997 and refers to a simple web page consisting of brief paragraphs of opinion, information, personal diary entries, or links, called posts, arranged chronologically with the most recent first, in the style of an online journal. Most blogs also allow visitors to add a comment below a blog entry. Blogs are two-way web-based communication tools with whose help anyone can enter their thoughts and comments to be seen by a limited group or by the whole web community. A blog is the simplest way to keep your own web site in the form of a diary. Besides text, a blog entry can include images, links, and even videos. Blogs are created by using one of the many blogging softwares, e.g. Blogger which is owned by Google.

Wikis: A wiki is a webpage or set of WebPages that can be easily edited by anyone who is allowed access. Wikipedia's popular success has meant that the concept of the wiki, as a collaborative tool that facilitates the production of a group work, is widely understood. Wiki pages have an edit button displayed on the screen and the user can click on this to access an easy-to-use online editing tool to change or even delete the contents of the page in question. Simple, hypertext-style linking between pages is used to create a navigable set of pages.

Tagging and social book marking: A tag is a keyword that is added to a digital object (e.g. a website, picture or video clip) to describe it, but not as part of a formal classification system. One of the first large-scale applications of tagging was seen with the introduction of Joshua Schacter's del.icio.us website, which launched the 'social bookmarking' phenomenon.

Social bookmarking systems share a number of common features: They allow users to create lists of 'bookmarks' or 'favourites', to store these centrally on a remote service (rather than within the client browser) and to share them with other users of the system (the 'social' aspect). These bookmarks can also be tagged with keywords, and an important difference from the 'folder'- based categorisation used in traditional, browser-based bookmark lists is that a bookmark can belong in more than one category.

Multimedia sharing: One of the biggest growth areas has been amongst services that facilitate the storage and sharing of multimedia content. Well known examples include YouTube (video) Flickr (photographs) and Odeo (podcasts). Literally millions of people now participate in the sharing and exchange of these forms of media by producing their own podcasts, videos and photos. This development has only been made possible through the widespread adoption of high quality, but relatively low cost digital media technology such as hand-held video cameras.

Audio blogging and podcasting: Podcasts are audio recordings, usually in MP3 format, of talks, interviews and lectures, which can be played either on a desktop computer or on a wide range of handheld MP3devices. Originally called audio blogs they have their roots in efforts to add audio streams to early blogs. Once standards had settled down and Apple introduced the commercially successful iPod MP3 player and its associated iTunes software, the process started to become known as podcasting. This term is not without some controversy since it implies that only the Apple iPod will play these files, whereas, in actual fact, any MP3 player or PC with the requisite software can be used. A more recent development is the introduction of video podcasts (sometimes shortened to vidcast or vodcast): the online delivery of video-on-demand clips that can be played on a PC, or again on a suitable handheld player (the more recent versions of the Apple iPod for example, provide for video playing).

Social Networking: Web 2.0 has changed the ways in which especially technology oriented and young people communicate. Community and social networking applications offer inspiration to action, ways of expressing oneself, and ways of communicating with others. It has also been stated that social web enhances human connectivity and sociability. Virtual communities and social networks make it possible for anyone to find people with same kinds of interests. Web communication tools have become more important than phone to some people. Social networking applications often require a log in and the creation of your own user profile. There have been several social networking success stories in recent years. Applications, such as Face book, MySpace, and Twitter, fall into the category of world's most popular web sites. These applications are used e.g. for forming and managing social capital and for intensifying offline relationships.

e-mail: Electronic mail, commonly called email or e-mail, is a method of exchanging digital messages across the Internet or other computer networks. Originally, email was transmitted directly from one user to another computer. This required both computers to be online at the same time. Today's email systems are based on a store-and-forward model. Email servers accept, forward, deliver and store messages. Users no longer need be online simultaneously and need only connect briefly, typically to an email server, for as long as it takes to send or receive messages. An email message consists of two components, the message ***header***, and the message ***body***, which is the email's content. The message header contains control information, including, minimally, an originator's email address and one or more recipient addresses. Usually additional information is added, such as a subject header field.

4.

Pedagogy

Instructional Technology

Instructional Technology is neither technology in education nor technology of education but both and all pervasive which pervades the whole teaching-learning process to make it meaningful for the teacher who teaches and the learner who learns and modifies his behaviour for his own betterment and the betterment of mankind. Instructional technology should not be confused with teaching or instruction or education or learning or engineering but it should be taken as a sum of all such aspects, which go a long way in shaping the personality of the learner in a meaningful context. It is an aggressive invention in education which has a promising future in the hands of all those who are constantly engaged in the pursuit of knowledge.

Definitions of Instructional Technology

The important definitions of instructional technology are:

1. Instructional technology is the application of scientific knowledge and learning and the conditions of learning to improve the effectiveness and efficiency teaching and training. –G.O. Leith
2. Instructional Technology is the form detailed application of psychology of learning to practice teaching problems. –John P. Detecco
3. Instructional Technology may be defined as the application of the laws as well as recent discoveries of science and technology to the process of education. – S.S. Kulkarni

4. Instructional Technology is that branch of educational theory and practice concerned primarily with the design and use of massages which control the learning process. -E.E. Hadden
5. Instructional Technology is the application of scientific process to man's learning conditions. -Robert A. Cox

Objectives of Instructional Technology

1. To identify the educational needs and aspirations of the community.
2. To determine the aims, objectives and in general the structure of education.
3. To develop an integrated curriculum of arts, science and human values.
4. To identify and locate material resources and strategies for achieving the desired aims of education.
5. To develop specific models of teaching to bring about an improvement in the teaching-learning process.
6. To design, modify and develop appropriate equipment/aids suitable and relevant to the educational process.

Scope of Instructional Technology

Educational technology aims to improve the quality of human learning. Educational technology is a field involved in applying a complex integrated process to analyse and solves problems in human learning. The scope of educational technology is unlimited as it tries to reach out to more and more people involved in the teaching-learning process.

The scope of educational technology is as follows:

- *Spelling out Educational Goals and Objectives:* Educational technology as a discipline strives for the formulation of objectives and goals of education based on individual and societal needs.

- ***Curriculum Development*:** Planning of curricular and co-curricular inputs in order to realise planned goals and objectives. It also highlights ways and means of content selection, transaction and sequencing of teaching-learning activities.
- ***Developing Teaching – Learning Materials and Resources:*** Programmed learning books, computer learning packages, mass media instructions, individualised self instructional package etc.
- ***Developing Human Resources:*** Strategies like team-teaching, models of teaching, training techniques like microteaching and simulated teaching and classroom interaction analysis.
- ***Developing Tactics and Strategies:*** In this area different teaching strategies, approaches and methods are devised and developed catering to different types of students.
- ***Development Multi-sensory Aids:*** The hardware aspect caters to the design, fabrication and development of audiovisual aids. Under its purview the selection, usage and storage of audiovisual aids also features.
- ***Feedback Mechanism and Modification:*** Educational Technology has a grip over the entire teaching-learning process. It develops tools of evaluation to provide feedback. On the basis of feedback mechanisms modifications in the process are incorporated.
- ***Develops Learning Environment:*** Educational Technology develops environments that are learner friendly. Simulations are a good example.
- ***Develops Information Resources:*** Today, Educational Technology is bridging the gap between developments in Information Technology and Education. Emergences of e-Libraries, Internet WWW, etc., have revolutions information resources.

Need of Educational Technology

1. ***Increasing the Effectiveness of Teaching-Learning Process:*** it brings desired improvement in teaching -learning process by making it effective. It develops to the maximum the cognitive, affective and psychomotor aspects of the pupils.
2. ***Maximising the Output:*** It has maximised the learning facilities. It is because it used the principles indoctrinated by Psychology, Sociology, Mathematics, Engineering and other social and scientific subject. Their input maximizes their output in the form of their competency by this technology.
3. ***Optimum use of Resources:*** The developing countries possess very limited resources. They lack experts, machinery or tools, school building, stationery and time. Educational technology emphasizes the maximum use of available resources in the learning situations, which may benefit all the pupils of the nation from those limited resources which are available for teaching work pertaining to this task.
4. Population Explosion.
5. Rapid Generation of New Knowledge
6. Development of new Strategies.
7. Controlled Atmosphere.
8. Importance of the Teacher Role.
9. Mass extension of Model Teaching
10. Beneficial for Teacher Training Colleges.
11. Improvement of School administration.
12. Preservation of teaching models.
13. Creation of interesting learning situations.

Concept/Components of Educational Technology

Educational Technology is considered to be the intermix of two aspects:

(*i*) Technology of Education and

(*ii*) Technology in Education

Technology of Education: It is nothing but techniques and methodologies of the teaching-learning process. This is indeed the software aspect of educational technology. The origin of software is closely associated with the courseware, i.e., instructional design and development of a subject.

Technology in Education: It signifies the use of audiovisual equipment, i.e., hardware in educational process.

TYPES OF EDUCATIONAL TECHNOLOGY

Lumsdane suggests that educational technology has the following three forms:

(A) Educational Technology I (or) Hardware Approach,

(B) Educational Technology II (or) Software Approach,

(C) Educational Technology III (or) Systems Approach.

(A) Hardware Approach

This approach implies the use of mechanical materials and equipment in education. Silverman says that this type of educational technology had its origin in physical sciences and engineering and is based on the concept of service i.e., using technology or instrumentation in the process of education. This approach is a by product of the scientific and technological development of the 20th Century.

In this approach the main feature is the use of audiovisual aids like charts, models, filmstrips, sliders, audiocassettes and sophisticated equipments and gadgets like film projectors, overhead projector, slide projectors, radio, tape recorder, LCD, CD players, television, computer etc. Most of these gadgets were not designed for the use in education but now have wide ranging applications in the teaching-learning process. This approach involves the entrance of technology from outside and hence it operates in isolation.

(B) Software Approach

The hardware approach has its origins in the field of physical science and engineering. In contrast, the software approach owes its origin to the behavioural sciences and their applied aspects concerned with psychology of learning. Arthur Melton says that software teaching technology is directly related to the psychology of learning which comprises behavioural changes resulting from experience. Davis associates software approach with the modern principles of programmed learning and says that it is characterized by task analysis, writing precise objectives, selection of appropriate learning strategies, reinforcement of correct responses and constant evaluation. The aspects which come under software approach are models of teaching, programmed learning, microteaching, strategies like team teaching, action analysis teacher, CAI, CAL and CML etc.

(C) System Approach

System analysis is also known as Management Technology. Developed after World War - II, it provided a scientific basis to the decision making regarding the problems associated with administration, management, commerce, industry and army. It helps to study the problems of educational administration and management in a scientific and conclusive way. By using it we can make the educational system, educational administration and management effective. It helps in the development of educational administration and formulation of instructional outline. Educational system, educational administration and management can be made more effective and less costly by using it. Hence these days the system approach occupies an important place in the field of teaching.

Difference between Hardware and Software Approach

S.No.	*Hardware Approach*	*Software Approach*
1.	***Origin***: From physical science and applied engineering	***Origin***: From behavioural sciences and applied aspects concerning psychology of learning.
2.	***Nomenclature***: Media Technology	***Nomenclature***: Instructional or teaching technology
3.	***Effect on teaching:*** Mechanises teaching	***Effect on teaching***: Improves the effectiveness and efficiency of teaching learning.
4.	***Inputs***: Mechanical devices which were commercially prepared like Radio/T.V. are used	***Inputs:*** Materials are prepared keeping in view learner needs. Specifically for the purpose of education.
5.	***Overall concept***: It is more concerned with the use of audiovisual material and sophisticated instruments, gadgets and teacher to achieve better results, lowering costs and reaching out to more students	***Overall concept:*** It tries to make use of psychology of learning for the production and utilization of software techniques and materials, teaching-learning strategies etc. to soften and smoothen task of teaching learning.
6.	***Teaching tearing:*** Hardware devices since the material used in their making is a relatively hard material and operation and working is somewhat technical and complex to handle.	***Teaching tearing:*** Software materials are relatively soft and delicate to handle.

Application of Educational Technology

Educational technology developed as a new subject in the field of education during the last few years. The term 'Education' includes teaching, learning, instruction and training.

In schools Educational Technology has its application in the following general working areas:

- ***Curriculum Construction***: In the present technological and psychological age, the application of scientific and technological knowledge is much essential for the curriculum construction. The curriculum construction has become a very tedious job in the field of education. It can be simplified with the help of educational technology.
- ***Selection of Teaching-Learning Strategies***: The selection of teaching-learning strategies turns easy with the help of educational technology.
- ***Selection of Audio-Visual Material***: Another important working area of educational technology is that the teacher can select easily the audio-visual aids with its assistance.
- ***Determination of Educational Objectives***: The software aspect of educational technology contributes in the formulation of teaching objectives.
- ***Teachers Training***: The new innovations in educational technology can be used successfully in teachers' training and it is actually being done, such as micro-teaching, simulated teaching, system approach, classroom interaction and teaching models etc.
- ***Feedback***: In the field of education, educational technology has emphasised on feedback for evaluation. Many experiments have been carried out in this area.
- ***Hardwares***: One form of educational technology also occurs as hardware devices such as teaching machines, tape-recorder, television, computer and satellite etc. the learning in the classroom can be made effective with their use.

Role of Educational Technology

Educational technology plays a significant role in present educational context. They are :

1. Converting behavioural objectives into the learning conditions in the context of educational objectives.
2. Analysing the characteristics of the learners.
3. Organizing the contents.
4. Formulating or constructing the media of presenting the contents.
5. Evaluating the performance of the pupils with reference to the achievement of educational objectives.
6. Providing reinforcement and feedback in order to modify the behaviours of the pupils.

TEACHING AND INSTRUCTION

Teaching is an intimate contact between a more mature personality and a less mature one which is designed to further the education of later. *-H.C. Morrison (1943)*

Teaching is the means whereby the experienced members of the group guide the immature and infant members in their adjustment of life. *-Yoakum and Simson*

Difference between Teaching and Instruction

In order to understand the real meaning of teaching, it is essential to understand the difference between teaching and instruction. Hence, we are clarifying the differences in these two terms in the following lines.

Teaching: Teaching is a kind of mentoring. In teaching, an interaction occurs between the teacher and the pupils. As a result of which the pupils are diverted towards the objectives. In other words, the main element of teaching i.e. the mutual relationship or the interaction between the teacher and the pupils advances the pupils towards objectives.

Instruction: The instruction does not involve an interaction between the teacher and the pupils. Still in instruction can divert the pupils towards objectives. The main difference between teaching and instruction is that the teaching includes instruction but the instruction does not include teaching. Hence, the teaching is instruction but the instruction is not teaching. In spite of this, all the three cognitive, affective and psychomotor aspects of the pupils can be developed by teaching, while by instruction; only cognitive aspect can be developed. Hence, no instruction can replace the teaching. In short, instruction is that process which diverts the pupils towards the objectives of cognitive aspect.

LECTURE METHOD

The lecture is still the most frequently used method of instruction. However, presenting a lecture without pausing for interaction with trainees can be ineffective regardless of your skill as a speaker. The use of pauses during the lecture for direct oral questioning creates interaction between instructor and trainee. Unfortunately, when classes are large, the instructor cannot possibly interact with all trainees on each point. The learning effectiveness of the lecture method has been questioned because of the lack of interaction; but it continues as a means of reaching a large group at one time with a condensed, organized body of information. Providing trainees with lesson objectives before the lecture will enable them to listen more effectively. It will help them to take concise, brief notes concerning the objectives rather than writing feverishly throughout the lecture.

It is one of the oldest methods of training. This method is used to create understanding of a topic or to influence behaviour, attitudes through lecture. A lecture can be in printed or oral form. Lecture is telling someone about something. Lecture is given to enhance the knowledge of listener or to give him the theoretical aspect of a topic. Training is basically incomplete without lecture. When the trainer begins the training session by telling the aim, goal, agenda, processes, or methods that will be used in training that means the trainer is using the lecture method. It is difficult to imagine training without lecture format. There are some variations in Lecture method. The variation here means that some forms of lectures are interactive while some are not.

The lecture is one of the oldest and basic methods of teaching. Although experience and educational researches have shown that the lecture is less effective than activity methods at school level, we find that most science teachers spend nearly 50 percent or more of their time lecturing. The use of lecturing depends on the subject matter, teaching philosophy of teacher and overall learning situation. Formal lecturing is used largely to build of basic theoretical knowledge, which must be gained before practice of skills. If the number of students in a class is large, teaching resources are scarce or time available is limited, lecturing appears to be the only way out.

Carter Good defines a lecture as "an instruction procedure by which the lecturer seeks to create interest to influence, stimulate or mould opinion, to promote activity, to impart information, or to develop critical thinking, largely by the use of the verbal message, with a minimum of class participation; illustrations, maps, charts or other visual aids may be employed to supplement the oral technique."

Steps in a Lecture Method

That the three main stages in any educational activity are planning, presentation and conclusion. Following figure represents the steps under lecture method.

Lecturer Method	Planning stage	Determining the aim of lecture Formulation of objectives of lecture Preparing the outline of body of lecture.
	Presentation of the lecture	Discussion Demonstration Illustration Examples
	Conclusions	Questions summarising

Characteristics of a Good Lecture

The characteristics of a good lecture are

- In the lecture method, the teacher plays a pivotal role and is the active participant.
- In a lecture method flow of the subject is retained.
- An enthusiastic lecturer is one who is well organised, challenging and clear in his presentation.
- The presentation includes an overview, logical organization and closure.
- The organization of the lecture should be explicit to the audience, so that they understand the relationship between various parts.
- Use of verbal clues and visual aids enhance the lecture
- Attention and motivation is sustained through use of anecdotes, physical activity, humour etc.
- The student is challenged to become intellectually involved with the topic being presented.
- The students are attracted towards an interesting lecture if the interest in the topic is developed.

Advantages of Lecture Method

The advantages of lecture method are:

- The lecture method is the most economical way of getting a large amount of information across to a large class. A teacher can convey the information in a minimum time, thus enabling the syllabus to be covered within a stimulated time. It is economical in terms of money and time.
- The lecture is useful in imparting factual information in an efficient manner to convey facts to students who have difficulty in reading their texts.
- The lecture helps to channelise the thinking of students in a given direction.

- Some abstract topics in science are best taught by the lecture method. The teacher through tact, style and presentation can get his/her message through effectively.
- It gives a sense of fulfilment as regards the progress of the subject both to the teacher and the taught.
- The teacher is always alert and the most convenient method for the teacher is the lecture method.

Limitations of Lecture Method

The main limitations of the lecture method are:

- Science as we all know is more than a body of knowledge. Hence mere pouring information is psychologically unsound and leads to neglect of development of skills.
- Science is best learning by doing. There is no provision for activities in this method as students are passive.
- A poorly planned, poorly delivered lecture fails to motivate the students.
- Lecture method doesn't cater to the affective and psychomotor domains.
- A teacher needs a lot of prior knowledge to prepare a lecture.
- A teacher becomes an 'orator' rather than a 'teacher'.
- If student is not attentive he fails to grasp the lecture.

Techniques to maintain students' attention in a lecture setting are:

- Avoid direct repetition of material in a textbook so that it remains a useful alternative resource.
- Use paradoxes, puzzles and apparent contradictions to engage students.
- Make connections to current events and everyday phenomena.

- Begin each class by summarizing the main points you have made.
- End each class by summarizing the main points you have made.
- Adopt a reasonable and adjustable pace that balances content coverage and student understanding.
- Consider using slides, videos, films, CD-ROMs and computer simulations to enhance presentations, but remember that: Students cannot take notes in darkened rooms/The text needs to be large enough to read from the back of the room.
- Maintain eye contact with students in all parts of the room.
- Step out from behind the lecture bench when feasible.
- Move around, but not so much that it is distracting.
- Talk to the students, not the blackboard.
- While using the board, avoid blocking it with A.V.projectors or screens.
- Shift the mood and intensity.
- Vary presentations techniques.

The blackboard can be used to highlight important aspects of lecture. Care should be taken regarding generalisations. Involvement of students can make 'lecture' an effective took for higher classes.

Lecture with PowerPoint Presentation

Using PowerPoint as you lecture can be an effective way to help students learn the lessons that you are teaching. A large number of students learn best visually, so adding visual cues during your lecture is a good way to reach the visual learners in your class. Using PowerPoint as you lecture can also make your lectures more fun, which can result in making them more memorable.

Instructions

- Brainstorm ways that visual cues could enhance your lectures. For example, provide bulleted lists to coincide with the headings or parts of your lectures.
- Create a PowerPoint presentation to enhance your lectures. Use the best ideas from your brainstorming session as a starting point for your PowerPoint presentation. Keep the text minimal—just enough to prompt students to remember what you said during your lecture.
- Add graphics to your PowerPoint presentation. Most slides should include a graphic that enhances the text. Use the same graphic for the same ideas, such as a key each time you present "key points" from the lecture. If you use the same graphic consistently for the same message, it will serve as a visual cue for the students and help them connect the ideas you have presented.
- Make the PowerPoint presentation interesting. Inject some humor into your presentation where appropriate. Using appropriate humor can help hold your students' attention.
- Set up an LCD projector. An LCD (liquid crystal display) projector will project your PowerPoint presentation onto the wall or a screen so that all of your students can view the PowerPoint presentation during your lecture.
- Display the PowerPoint presentation as you lecture. If you have included a slide for every topic, then your students will associate what you said with the slides that you projected during that part of the lecture.
- Print out handouts of the PowerPoint slides and distribute them to your class. Students will get a big picture view of the lecture but be responsible for filling in the details. Looking at the handouts of the slides will help your students remember your lecture.

Ten Secrets for Using PowerPoint Effectively

Here are ten secrets based on years of experience in developing and using presentation slides that will help you move from being technically proficient to using PowerPoint effectively.

1. Use the Outline View first: The most important part of any presentation is the content, not the graphical appeal. That is why you should develop your presentation with the content first, before deciding on the look (colours, graphics, etc.) The best way to do this is to use the Outline view. This view is accessed by clicking on the View menu and selecting the Outline command or by clicking on the Outline tool button at the bottom left of the screen (the one with all the lines). This view only shows the text of each slide. You use the Tab key to move to a lower level within a slide or the Shift-Tab key to move to a higher level in the slide. By using the Outline View first, you ensure that the content of your presentation is solid before you concern yourself with the visual elements.
2. Use Contrasting Colours: If you want your audience to be able to see what you have on the slide, there needs to be a lot of contrast between the text colour and the background colour.
3. Use a big enough font: When deciding what font size to use in your presentation, make sure it is big enough so that the audience can read it. Usually find that any font size less than 24 point is too small to be reasonably read in most presentation situations. The programmers would prefer to see most text at a 28 or 32 point size, with titles being 36 to 44 point size. The only reason they would use a font less than 24 point is when adding explanatory text to a graph or diagram, where you could use a 20 point font size. If you are given a small screen in a big room, your font will look smaller because the image will not be as big

as it should be. In this case, see if you can get a larger screen, use a wall instead of a screen to project on, move the chairs closer to the screen or remove the last few rows of chairs.

4. Stop the moving text: When text comes on the screen, we want the audience to read the text, then focus back on the presenter to hear the message. If the text moves onto the screen in any way - such as flying in, spiral or zooming - it makes it harder for the audience members to read since they have to wait until the text has stopped before they can read it. This makes the presenter wait longer between each point and makes the audience members focus more on the movement than on what is being said

5. Turn the pointer off: During a presentation, it is very annoying to have the pointer (the little arrow) come on the screen while the presenter is speaking. It causes movement on the screen and draws the audience attention from the presenter to the screen. The pointer comes on when the mouse is moved during the presentation. To prevent this from happening, after the Slide Show view has started, press the Ctrl-H key combination. This prevents mouse movement from showing the pointer. If you need to bring the pointer on screen after this, press the A key. If the pointer does appear during your presentation, resist the urge to press the Escape key - if you do, it will stop the presentation and drop you back into the program. Press the A key or Ctrl-H to make the pointer disappear.

6. Use visuals instead of text slides: The latest survey confirms that audiences are more fed up than ever with the overload of text on slides. Instead of using slides that only contain text, use visuals such as graphs, diagrams, photos and media clips to engage the audience.

7. Have Slides at the End of Your Presentation: The last slide you speak to should not be the last slide in your presentation file. You should have three identical copies of your last speaking slide so that if you accidentally advance one too many times at the end of your presentation, your audience never knows because you don't drop into the program, the slide looks like it has not changed. After these slides, you should include some slides that answer questions that you expect to be asked. These slides will be useful during Q&A sessions after the presentation. The final slide should be a blank slide so that if you go through all the other slides, you have a final backup from dropping into the program.
8. Be able to Jump to Any Slide: PowerPoint has a feature that allows you to be able to move quickly and seamlessly to any slide in your presentation. To do so, you need to know the slide numbers. The easiest way to print a list of the slide numbers and associated slide titles is to go to the Outline View and collapse the details for each slide. Then print the view. To jump to any slide, just enter the slide number on the keyboard and press the Enter key. This will move you directly to that slide. This technique is very useful for moving to a prepared Q and A slide or for skipping parts of your presentation if time becomes an issue.
9. Blank the screen: Sometimes we want the image on the screen to disappear so that the audience is focused solely on the presenter. There are two ways to do this. The first is if you want to blank the screen with a black image, similar to shutting the projector off (we used to do this all the time with overhead projectors by just shutting the projector off). Just press the B key on the keyboard and the image is replaced with a black image. Press the B key again and the image is restored. If you want to use a white image instead of a black image, press the W key each time.

10. Draw on the screen during a presentation: Sometimes it can be valuable to be able to draw on the screen during your presentation to illustrate a particular point or item. This can be done in the following way. Press the Ctrl-P key combination to display a pen on the screen. Then, using the left mouse button, draw on the slide as you wish. To erase what you have drawn, press the E key. To hide pen, press the A key or the Ctrl-H key combination.

When you employ these secrets to use PowerPoint effectively, you will greatly enhance your audience's understanding of your message and help to make your presentation the best it can be.

Creating a Successful Presentation

There are diverse teaching and learning contexts in which PowerPoint can be used for presentations but the key general requirements are summarised below:

- Plan your presentation structure carefully and according to the general rules of presentations. The key to a successful presentation/lecture is to have a clear structure and generally not more than five key topic areas.
- Know the level at which the presentation is aimed and develop the content for that level.
- Do not present too much textual material on each slide and avoid simply reading out what is on the slide: provide mainly structural headings and sub-headings around which the bulk of the verbal presentation takes place so that students still require to be active and take notes of details.
- Make sure that you speak at a normal pace and do not allow the use of PowerPoint to deliver material too quickly: this is one of the most commonly encountered problems when converting to use PowerPoint.

- Utilise the visual and other media opportunities offered to enhance your presentation whenever possible but be careful to avoid excessive use of colour effects, animation effects, transition effects, sound effects, etc.

There are many varied sources of information on the do's and don'ts of constructing and delivering PowerPoint presentations but one of the most useful is that found at Presenters University where you can also acquire a collection of free templates suitable for many different forms of presentations, including educational. Some key points relating to designing PowerPoint presentations are given below:

- Try to avoid having more than 6 lines of text per slide and make them primarily headings or subheadings.
- Remember that a picture can be worth a thousand words (Beakes, 2003) – use graphics to enhance your presentation. Consider how you can make such diagrams available to the students (time to copy during presentation, handouts, files, etc.) but be aware of copyright limitations on non-original material.
- Try to avoid using red and green combinations for emphasis – the most common form of colour blindness prevents separation of reds and greens.
- Consider introducing lines of text one at a time, dimming the previous lines as the new line is introduced: this facilitates concentration on the current item. Putting the full slide up can result in the audience reading ahead and not listening to what is being currently discussed. This facility is accessed within the custom animation option.
- Standardise on a form of animated text entry that is straightforward: I use 'wipe right' since I consider that it mimics the normal entry of text in a word processor and feels natural, at least for those from most western countries.

- Use a Sans Serif font such as Arial rather than a Serif font such as Times New Roman: typographical texts recommend this as being easier to read on a poster or presentation slide. If you want a more casual font, Comic Sans is a popular alternative. For reading from paper handouts, etc., a Serif font is recommended.
- Do not use more than two text colours in a presentation unless there are particular reasons for doing so.
- Consider whether to use a dark or a light background for the presentation. Dark backgrounds may not work well if the room is not fairly dark. Remember that too darker the room has to be; the more likely the audience are to find it hard to stay awake!
- Bear in mind that students with dyslexia often find high contrast between text and background (such as black text on white background) very difficult to read. Consider standardising on reduced contrast combinations (e.g. yellow text on dark blue background) for that reason.

Reasons to use PowerPoint

So why should you consider using PowerPoint for your teaching and learning activities? There are many reasons but the key ones include:

- Appropriate use of PowerPoint can enhance the teaching and learning experience for both staff and students.
- It provides encouragement and support to staff by facilitating the structuring of a presentation in a professional manner. The templates provided have been designed to default to good presentation criteria such as the number of lines of information per slide and appropriate font sizes and types, etc: using the styles of the default templates can significantly improve clarity and structuring of a presentation. This

helps to avoid the common use of excessive text often found on overhead transparencies.

- By careful mixing of media, a presentation can appeal to a number of different learning styles and be made more stimulating. You are encouraged to incorporate more sophisticated visual and auditory media into presentations although care is required because of the inevitable increase in file sizes and the danger of excessive use. Incorporation can be done, either directly from within the programme or, sometimes more successfully, by appropriate pausing of the PowerPoint presentation and using alternative technology (e.g. Tape Recorder or VCR). Note that this does not require switching off either the computer system or the projector system, one of the most common perceptions that restrict use – instead, use the 'B' character toggle switch during a slide presentation to 'blank' the screen temporarily while using other media.
- The electronic file format allows distribution and modification for/by students unable to be present or who have impaired visual or auditory difficulties. PowerPoint comes with a free viewer programme that can be distributed with the files so that the reader is not required to have PowerPoint on their personal system. However, if they do have it, they are able to perform a greater variety of manipulations on the PowerPoint file provided, such as editing the text, etc before printing it out. Most Virtual Learning Environments (VLEs) are now capable of including PowerPoint presentations if required.

DEMONSTRATION METHOD

Use the demonstration or "doing" method to teach skills. Demonstrate, step-by-step, the procedures in a job task, using the exact physical procedures if possible. While demonstrating, explain the reason and the significance of each step. To be effective, plan the demonstration so that you will be sure to show steps in proper sequence and to include all steps.

If you give the demonstration before a large group or if the trainees might have trouble seeing because of the size of the equipment involved, use enlarged devices or training aids. When practical, allow trainees to repeat the procedure in a "hands on" practice session to reinforce the learning process. By immediately correcting the trainees' mistakes and reinforcing proper procedures, you can help them learn the task more quickly. The direct demonstration approach is a very effective method of instruction, especially when trainees have the opportunity to repeat the procedures.

Techniques Used in the Demonstration Method

The basic method of instruction for teaching skill-type subject matter is the demonstration-performance method of instruction. This method is recommended for teaching a skill because it covers all the necessary steps in an effective learning order.

The demonstration step gives trainees the opportunity to see and hear the details related to the skill being taught. Those details include the necessary background knowledge, the steps or procedure, the nomenclature, and the safety precautions. The repetition step helps the average and slow learners and gives the trainees an additional opportunity to see and hear the skill being taught. The performance step gives all trainees the opportunity to become proficient. In short, this method is recommended because it leaves nothing to chance.

For convenience, the techniques for imparting skills are presented in steps, rather than activities. When setting up an instructional plan, understand that you don't have to follow these steps in the sequence presented; instead choose the steps in the sequence best suited to the needs of the trainees. Although you will always include a demonstration step and a performance step, you must use judgment in selecting techniques to make the various steps effective.

Demonstration Step

Every Navy skill, mental or physical, has a body of background knowledge the trainees must know to perform the skill properly. You can best teach some kinds of background knowledge in a standard classroom with adequate, comfortable seating and the display of training aids. You will present other kinds of knowledge in ships or laboratories in conjunction with actual demonstrations.

Develop proper attitudes while teaching the skill. Developing the desire to do a perfect job, the desire to exercise economy of time and effort, and the desire to protect the lives of others are all important attitudes. Use a variety of techniques in presenting background knowledge and in developing proper attitudes. The following techniques relate more to the actual demonstration:

- Position the trainees and training aids properly. If you direct trainees to gather around a worktable or a training aid, make sure every trainee has an unobstructed view.
- Show and explain each operation. Perform each operation in step-by-step order. Whenever possible, give the instructions while you demonstrate. Do not hurry; don't emphasize speed in performing operations or in moving from one operation to another during the demonstration step. Make certain the trainees understand the first step before you proceed to the second step, and so on. Repeat difficult operations. Pause briefly after each operation to observe trainee reactions and to check trainee comprehension. In certain skills a distinction between right and left is important; for example, the manual of arms or knot tying. When teaching the manual of arms, or skills of a similar nature, use an assistant instructor or a well-coached trainee to demonstrate the skill while you give instructions. This method of instruction allows you to observe the reaction of the

trainees. Observe safety precautions. By observing safety precautions, you may take a few more seconds to rig a safety line, don a safety mask, or tag an electric cable; but the time is not wasted. You are impressing the trainees with the importance of exercising extreme care in dealing with potentially dangerous equipment.

- Give proper attention to terminology. Call each part of a training aid by its proper name each time you call attention to it. For trainees to remember the correct nomenclature, however, requires more than your use of the proper names of parts. The following suggestions should prove helpful: (a) List the names of parts on the chalkboard. (b) Refer trainees to any available chart that shows the parts and names of parts. (c) Conduct a terminology drill on the parts of the training aid while the aid is in its assembled or disassembled condition.
- Check trainee comprehension carefully. Ask questions during the demonstration step—questions that require the trainees to recall nomenclature, procedural steps, underlying principles, safety precautions, and the like. Watch for class reactions that show a lack of attention, confusion, or doubt; but do not depend solely upon visual observations. Instead, check comprehension after each major step or procedure.

Requirements of Good Demonstration

The success of any demonstration following points should be kept in mind.

- It should be planned and rehearsed by the teacher before hand.
- The apparatus used for demonstration should be big enough to be seen by the whole class. If the class may be disciplined she may allow them to sit on the benches to enable them a better view.

- Adequate lighting arrangements be made on demonstration table and a proper background table need to be provided.
- All the pieces of apparatus be placed in order before starting the demonstration. The apparatus likely to be used should be placed in the left hand side of the table and it should be arranged in the same order in which it is likely to be used.
- Before actually starting the demonstration a clear statement about the purpose of demonstration be made to the students.
- The teacher makes sure that the demonstration lecture method leads to active participation of the students in the process of teaching.
- The demonstration should be quick and slick and should not appear to linger on unnecessarily.
- The demonstration should be interesting so that it captures the attention of the students.
- It would be better if the teacher demonstrates with materials or things the children handles in everyday life.
- For active participation of students the teacher may call individual student in turn to help him in demonstration.
- The teacher should write the summary of the principles arrived at because of demonstration on the blackboard. The black board can be also used for drawing the necessary diagrams.

Lecture-Cum-Demonstration Method

The lecture and demonstration methods are interrelated and are combined to form lecture cum demonstration method. In this method the faults of the lecture method are removed and combined with the merits of demonstration method making the method impressive, economical and useful.

The teacher performs an experiment and goes on explaining what he does. It takes into account the active participation of the students and is thus not a completely lop-sided process like lecture method. The students see the actual apparatus and operations and help the teacher in demonstrating the experiment and thereby they are comparatively more interested in learning. It is difficult to talk about things the students have to imagine.

Steps in a lecture-Demonstration Method

Thus, in this method, the teacher explains the theoretical portion with the help of lecture method using blackboard, diagrams or chart etc. To make the theoretical part clear he performs and demonstrates relevant experiments ensuring active participation of students.

(1) Planning and preparation: A great care has to be taken by the teacher while planning and preparing his demonstration lesson. He should keep the following points in mind while preparing his lesson.

(*a*) Subject matter.

(*b*) Questions to be asked.

(*c*) Apparatus required for the experiment

If the classroom or lecture hall is large, consider whether students at the back will be able to see your demonstration. Look into videotaping the demonstration and projecting the image on a larger screen so that all of your students can see.

To achieve the above stated objective, the teacher should thoroughly go through books relevant to the lesson. After this he should prepare his lesson plan in which he should include the principles to be explained, a list of experiments to be demonstrated and the type of questions to be asked from the students. Before actually demonstrating the experiment to a class the experiment has to be rehearsed under the conditions prevailing in the classroom. Inspire of all the precautions, something may go wrong during the actual lesson, so reserve apparatus must be arranged. The apparatus should be arranged in a systematic order on the demonstration table.

*(2) **Introduction of the lesson*** : The lesson should start with proper motivation to the students. It is usually considered more useful to introduce a lesson in the form of a problem, which would make the students realise the importance of the topic. For example: The teacher can consider opening a soda bottle in a classroom and asking the question like – What did you observe? Have you seen any gas coming out of the bottle? At this stage the teacher can introduce the topic of carbon dioxide.

*(3) **Presentation*** : The method of presenting the subject matter is very important. A good teacher should present his lesson in an interesting manner. To make the lesson interesting the teacher need not be very rigid to confine himself within the prescribed course, rather he should make the lesson as much broad based as possible. For widening the scope of his lesson the teacher may think of various useful applications of the principles taught by him. He is also at liberty to quote examples and illustrations from other allied branches of science to make his lesson interesting. The life history and some interesting facts from the life of the great scientist whose name is associated with the topic under discussion can also be cited to make the lesson interesting.

Constant questions and answers should form part of every demonstration lesson. Questions and cross questions are essential for properly illuminating the principle being discussed. Questions need to be in such a way that their answers form a complete teaching unit. Though an effort should be made to encourage the students to answer a large number of questions, the teacher should provide the answers to such questions if students fail to answer some questions.

*(4) **Performance of Experiments*** : A good observer has been described as a person who has learned to use his senses of touch, sight, smell and hearing in an intelligent and alert

manner. Children should be made to observe what happens in experiments and be provide with opportunities to state their observations carefully. They should also be encouraged to explain what happens with reference to their problem. They should finally be allowed to generalise on the basis of their observations.

The demonstration experiment should be presented by the teacher in a systematic manner. He should work in a tidy, clean and orderly manner while demonstrating an experiment. Some of the important points to be kept in mind while demonstrating an experiment are as follows:

- Experiments should be simple and easy.
- The experiments must work and their results should be clear and striking.
- Experiments need to be properly spaced throughout the lesson.
- Some reserve apparatus must be present on the demonstration table.
- The demonstration apparatus has to store till it has to be used again.

(5) Blackboard Summary : A summary of important results and principles must be written on the blackboard. Use of blackboard should also be frequently made for drawing necessary sketches and diagrams. The blackboard summary should be written in a neat, clean and legible way. Blackboard summary is an index to a teacher's ability.

(6) Supervision : Students need to be asked to take the complete notes of the blackboard summary including the sketches and diagrams drawn. Such a record will be quite helpful to the students for learning his lesson. Such a summary will prove beneficial only if it has been copied correctly from the blackboard and to make sure that students are copying the blackboard summary properly, the teacher should check it by frequently going to the seats of the students.

Merits of Lecture Demonstration Method

Following are the merits of this method:

- It combines all the plus points of lecture and demonstration methods, eliminating shortcomings of lecture method.
- It is an economical method as compared to purely student centered approaches.
- It is a psychological method and students take active interest in teaching learning process.
- It leads students from concrete to abstract situation and thus is more psychological.
- It is a suitable method if the apparatus to be handled is costly and sensitive and such an apparatus is likely to damage if handled by students.
- This method can be safer if the experiments to be demonstrated are dangerous.
- It can be used successfully for all types of students.
- In this method such experiments which are difficult for students can be included.
- This method can be used to impart manual and manipulative skills to students.

Limitations of Lecture Demonstration Method

Some of the limitations of this method are as under:

- Since the teacher performs the experiment at his own pace, many students cannot comprehend the concept being clarified.
- It fails to impart training in scientific attitude.
- This method is not child centred, it makes no provision for individual difference. All types of students including slow learners and geniuses have to proceed with the same speed.

- In this method students many a time fail to observe many finer details of the apparatus used because they observe it form a distance.

Science teachers should encourage more direct experiments by children in order to help children broaden their range of fact-finding skills beyond the three T's- teacher, text book and television.

Common Errors in Demonstration Lesson

A summary of the common errors committed while delivering a demonstration lesson is Given below:

- Apparatus may not be ready for use
- There may not be an apparent relation between the demonstration experiment and the topic under discussion.
- Black board summary not up to the mark
- Teacher may be in a hurry to arrive at a generalisation without allowing students to arrive at a generalisation from facts.
- Teacher may take to talking too much which will affect the enthusiasm of the students.
- Teacher may not have allowed sufficient time for recording of data.
- Teacher may fail to ask the right type of questions.

TEACHING-LEARNING TECHNIQUES

Team Teaching

Team teaching is used to bring improvements in teaching-learning process. The present day education system has increased the responsibilities of the teacher. The teacher has to teach the same content every year. This develops alienation and disinterest in him. The need of team teaching arises in such conditions. In team teaching a group of teachers, working together, plan, conduct, and evaluate the learning activities for the same group of students. In practice, team teaching has many different formats but in general it is a means of organising staff into groups to enhance teaching. Teams generally comprise staff members who may represent different areas of subject expertise but who share the same group of students and a common planning period to prepare for the teaching. To facilitate this process a common teaching space is desirable. However, to be effective team teaching requires much more than just a common meeting time and space.

Team teaching was first developed in 1955 at Harvard University. In Britain, it was developed by J. Ereeman in 1960. Gradually, its use was started in schools and colleges. In Chicago University, Facis Chase used team teaching for effective teaching. After the successful application in colleges, the team-teaching was started for the training of the army during World War II. In India, this concept is being used but its success has been doubled.

Definition of Team Teaching

An instructional situation where two or more teachers possessing complementary teaching skills cooperatively plan and implement the instruction for a single group of students using flexible scheduling and grouping techniques to meet the particular instruction – *Carlo Olson*

Team teaching is a form of an organization in which teacher decide to post resources, interests and expertise in order to devise and implement the scheme of work suitable to the need of their pupils and facilities of their school.

– *David Warwick*

Characteristics of Team Teaching

- It is a teaching method.
- Two or more teachers participate in the teaching.
- The needs of the pupils and schools and existing resources are also considered.

- Various aspects of any topic of one subject is taught by two or more teachers turn by turn.
- The main objective is to make the teaching-learning more effective.
- Isolation among the teachers is removed.
- The teachers decide their activities themselves.
- It is a technique of creating instructional conditions.
- Its plan is flexible.
- It is based on cooperation. All the teachers participating in the team teaching apply their resources, abilities and experiences.

Principles of Team Teaching

- *Time factor:* The duration should be decided on the basis of subject's importance. To allot much time to an unimportant subject makes the team teaching ineffective.
- *Level of instruction:* Before imparting instruction to the pupils, the initial behaviours of the learners must be observed and the level of the instruction should be according to the pupils.
- *Supervision:* The type and the method of supervision depends upon the objectives of the group. Therefore, the objectives of the group must be kept in mind at the time of supervision.
- *Size and Composition:* The fixed size of the class is an old story now. In the present times the size of the group changes according to the objective of the team-teaching. Therefore, the size and composition of the group of the pupils should be appropriate according to the objectives of the group and learning experiences.
- *Appropriate duties assigned to teachers:* The division of duties and responsibilities of the teachers should

be appropriate. These duties should be assigned to them according to their academic merit, interests and their personality traits. Hence, the team members should be selected very carefully.

- ***Provision of learning environment:*** The team teaching is successful only if a proper learning environment is provided, with provision of library, laboratory, workshop etc.

Types of Team Teaching

1. ***Single disciplinary team teaching:*** In such classification, teachers come from a single department. This arrangement is made for secondary and higher secondary classes. It is possible only if there is more than one teacher for one subject.
2. ***Inter-disciplinary team teaching:*** In this classification, a team of teachers of different subjects is formed such as teachers in Psychology, Philosophy and Sociology etc. Now the teaching task is organised very easily. Thus, team teaching encourages interdisciplinary teaching.
3. ***Inter Institutional team teaching:*** In such team teaching, specialists from various institutions are invited at every level and for every topic. This provision proves much useful where there is only one subject teacher. Such team-teaching encourages cooperative teaching. The effective use of this team-teaching becomes more possible in a city where there are more than one training institutions.

Procedure of Team Teaching

The team-teaching is organized according to objectives in the teaching-learning process. A systematic procedure is followed through following steps or phases.

Planning Phase: At this stage team teaching involves the following types of activities.

- Decision about the topic to be taught.
- Formulating objectives and writing them in behavioural terms
- Identifying the initial behaviour of the learner.
- Identifying the available men and material resources.
- Selection of the comprising team teacher, team leader and other professional and non-professional helping hands.
- Taking decision about the tentative schedule, the larder or small group teaching, the level of instruction and teaching strategies etc.
- Distributing responsibilities among the member of the team according to their interest and abilities.
- Taking decision about the means and ways of evaluating the learning outcomes.

Execution Phase: Following activities are performed while organizing team teaching.

- Teacher asks some initial questions to decide the level of the instruction. Only then he can set the level of the instruction.
- Keeping in view the pupils' knowledge of the language, the communication technique is selected.
- Then other teachers of the team also deliver lecturers and clarify various elements.
- Pupils' activities are reinforced. The teacher encourages the students.
- The pupils are asked to perform certain tasks in the class during these lecturers.

Evaluation Phase: In this step, the evaluation occurs with the reference to the achievement of objectives on the basis of performances of the pupils. It is examined whether the objectives have been achieved or not. The following activities are performed in this step.

- Decision is taken regarding the achievement of objectives and performances by the pupils.
- Necessary modifications are introduced in the planning and execution phase on the basis of evaluation.
- For evaluation, oral and written questions and practical methods are followed. Each question evaluates some objective.
- The shortcoming and problems of the pupils are diagnosed and remedied.

Advantages of Team Teaching

- *Better quality of instruction:* The main utility of team teaching is the improvement in the quality of instruction.
- *Economical:* Team teaching is economical in terms of time and energy.
- *Discipline:* It also helps in maintaining the discipline in the class.
- *Exposure of group to more specialists:* The pupils can have maximum opportunities of facing maximum specialists. Hence, they gain the advantage of specific knowledge of the different teachers.
- *Development of Human Relation:* Human relations are very essential for social adjustment. Traditional teaching lack human relations. Team-teaching provides opportunities of developing human relations.
- *Opportunity for Free Discussion:* Team-teaching provides many opportunities to the member students for participating in the discussion. It provides stimulus to the ideas of the pupils and teachers.
- *Flexibility:* The school building staff and other resources of the school can be used very flexibly. Team teaching helps in getting rid off traditional time table.

- ***Will and responsibility:*** It develops strong will and responsibility of participating among the pupils and teachers.

Limitations of Team Teaching

- ***Costly method:*** Team learning is costlier than the traditional teaching. Its cost per head is more than that of the traditional teaching.
- ***Lack of cooperation:*** The basis of the team teaching is cooperation. But sometimes teachers hesitate to cooperate with other teachers. Hence, in team teaching cooperation from all the teachers cannot be expected.
- ***Lack or research work:*** Being a new concept, team teaching lacks research work. It is being used on the basis of trial and error method.
- ***Disregard to the dynamics of small group:*** No specific type of guidance can be imparted in team-teaching because school staff cannot function like a football team.

GROUP DISCUSSION

In its simple meaning, the term group discussion stands for the discussion held within a group. In this sense discussion as teaching strategy may be defined as some sort of discussion. i.e interchange of ideas between students and the teacher or among a group of students resulting into active learning for the realisation of the predetermined teaching learning objectives. This group discussion, in no way, occurs occasionally or incidentally but is planned and organised with deliberate efforts on the part of the teacher and student for achieving the set goals.

The Organizational Procedure of Group Discussion

In this strategy, students of a class may form a group along with the subject teacher. The teacher is the leader of this group on account of his status, functions and responsibilities fulfilled by him in the organization of group discussion. Usually the following three stages and steps are involved in the employment of group discussion as a teaching strategy.

1. Planning and setting the proper stage for discussion: The teacher induces the need of holding group discussion and sets the stage to make necessary assignment for facilitating the employment of group discussion as a teaching strategy.

2. Ensuring active, democratic and useful participation of the group members: At the second stage an environment for the proper implementation of the strategy is ensured. Teacher at this stage makes ensure that every member of the group plays active role in the group discussion. The discussions are held in a perfectly democratic style providing full and free exchange of ideas within the group. Teacher as a group leader controls and monitors the progress of the discussion in a perfectly democratic way with his least involvement in the discussion. The aim remains to make the members engaged in useful discussion for achieving the desired teaching learning objectives.

3. Evaluating the outcomes of the discussion in the light of the realisation of objectives: At the third stage, the outcomes of the discussion are evaluated in terms of the realization of the set objectives. For this purpose, a member secretary may be asked to kept the record of the discussion held in the group, the question raised, the suggestions put forth by the members, the efforts made and consensus reached, the direction and guidance given by the teacher as a group leader and conclusion arrived, are all noted.

Group Discussion Components

A Group Discussion Consists of :

1. Communication Skills
2. Knowledge and ideas regarding a given subject
3. Capability to co-ordinate and lead
4. Exchange of thoughts

5. Addressing the group as a whole
6. Thorough preparations

Communication Skills: The first aspect is one's power of expression. In a group discussion, a candidate has to talk effectively so that he is able to convince others. For convincing, one has to speak forcefully and at the same time create an impact by his knowledge of the subject. A candidate who is successful in holding the attention of the audience creates a positive impact.

Knowledge and Ideas Regarding a Given Subject : Knowledge of the subject under discussion and clarity of ideas are important. Knowledge comes from consistent reading on various topics ranging from science and technology to politics. In-depth knowledge makes one confident and enthusiastic and this in turn, makes one sound convincing and confident.

Leadership and Coordinating Capabilities : The basic aim of a group discussion is to judge a candidate's leadership qualities. The examiner withdraws and becomes a silent spectator once the discussion starts. A candidate should display tactfulness, skill, understanding and knowledge on varied topics, enterprise, forcefulness and other leadership qualities to motivate and influence other candidates who may be almost equally competent.

Exchange of Thoughts: A group discussion is an exchange of thoughts and ideas among members of a group. These discussions are held for selecting personnel in organisations where there is a high level of competition. The number of participants in a group can vary between 8 and 15. Mostly a topic or a situation is given to group members who have to discuss it within 10 to 20 minutes.

Addressing the Group as a Whole : In a group discussion it is not necessary to address anyone by name. Even otherwise you may not know everyone's names. It better to address the group as a whole.

Thorough Preparation: Start making preparations for interview and group discussions right away, without waiting till the eleventh hour, this is, if and when called for them. Then the time left may not be adequate. It is important to concentrate on subject knowledge and general awareness. Hence, the prime need for thorough preparation. Remember, the competition is very tough. It may so happen that you are called for interviews and group discussions from three or four organizations but are not selected by any. The reason obviously lies that are not being well-prepared.

Do's and Don'ts of Group Discussion

1. ***Keep eye contact while speaking:*** Do not look at the evaluators only. Keep eye contact with every team member while speaking.
2. ***Initiate the GD:*** Initiating the GD is a big plus. But keep in mind - Initiate the group discussion only when you understood the GD topic clearly and have some topic knowledge. Speaking without proper subject knowledge is bad impression.
3. ***Allow others to speak:*** Do not interrupt anyone in-between while speaking. Even if you don't agree with his/her thoughts do not snatch their chance to speak. Instead make some notes and clear the points when it's your turn.
4. ***Speak clearly:*** Speak politely and clearly. Use simple and understandable words while speaking. Don't be too aggressive if you are disagreeing with someone. Express your feelings calmly and politely.
5. ***Make sure to bring the discussion on track:*** If by any means group is distracting from the topic or goal then simply take initiative to bring the discussion on the track. Make all group members aware that you all need to come to some conclusion at the end of the discussion. So stick to the topic.
6. ***Positive attitude:*** Be confident. Do not try to dominate anyone. Keep positive body language. Show interest in discussion.

7. ***Speak sensibly:*** Do not speak just to increase your speaking time. Don't worry even if you speak less. Your thoughts should be sensible and relevant instead of irrelevant speech.
8. ***Listen carefully to others:*** Speak less and listen more! Pay attention while others are speaking. This will make coherent discussion and you will get involved in the group positively. You will surely make people agree with you.
9. ***No need to go into much detail:*** Some basic subject analysis is sufficient. No need to mention exact figures while giving any reference. You have limited time so be precise and convey your thoughts in short and simple language.
10. ***Formal dressing:*** Do not take it casually. No fancy and funny dressing. You should be comfortable while speaking in group. Positive gesture and body language will make your work easy.

Advantages of Group Discussion

It ensures the active participation of the students in the process of teaching-learning.

- It trains the students for carrying out group activities and co-operative tasks. The qualities linked to proper social development and democratic livings are also developed with the adoption of this strategy.
- It provides opportunities to the students for imbibing the qualities of a good listener as well as effective leader. When a group member speaks others listen with patience, try to show respect for his opinion but at the same time they may also put up their own views in a quite democratic way.
- It provides good training for verbal communication, expression of ideas and creative and constructive thinking.

- A free and democratic discussion provides proper check over the wrong information, ideas and ways of problem solving.
- Enhances learning in both the affective and cognitive domains.
- It is both learner-centered and subject-centered.
- Stimulates learners to think about issues and problems.
- Encourages learners to exchange their own experiences, thereby making learning more active and less isolating.
- Provides the opportunity for sharing of ideas and concerns.
- Fosters positive peer support and feeling of belonging.
- Reinforces previous learning.

Disadvantages of Group Discussion

- Easy to digress from the topic.
- Shy learners may refuse to become involved or may need a great deal of encouragement to participate.
- Particularly challenging for the novice teacher when group members do not interact easily.
- More time consuming for the transmission of information than other methods such as lecture.
- Requires the teacher's presence at all sessions to act as a facilitator and resource person.
- One member of the group can dominate the discussion.

PANEL DISCUSSION TECHNIQUE

All techniques of higher learning require discussion among the participants, which provides equal opportunities to every participant in the instructional situation.

Panel discussion technique of learning is based on the modern theory of organization. It assumes that every member of the organization has the capacity to initiate and solve the problem and brings certain attitude and values to the organization. Thus, interactional technique is the most appropriate in democratic way of life.

Origin of Panel Discussion

For the first time this technique was used by Herry A Ober Street in 1929. He organized a discussion of a definite period for small group and the audience. At the end of the discussion audience also participated. Important questions were put by the audiences on the topic. The experts tried to answer the questions certain points were clarified, which were not included in the discussion.

Objectives of Panel Discussion

- To provide information and new facts
- To analyse the current problem form different angle.
- To identify the values
- To organise for mental recreation.
- To find out solution of current problem of important nature.
- To provide the full understanding of significant topic.
- To create situation to facilitate higher cognitive learning.

Characteristics of Panel Discussion

- It is used at college and university level to organise teaching at reflective level.
- It develops the ability of problem solving.
- It provides the opportunity to understand the problem or theme of the discussion.
- It develops ability of presentation of theme and logically giving their point of view.
- It develops the right type of attitude and the ability to tolerate anti-ideas of others.

- It develops the ability of creative thinking and criticising the theme.
- It develops the manners of putting questions and answering questions.

Types of Panel Discussion

Group discussion is organized in different forms, for different levels, for different purpose and on different themes as follows:

Pubic Panel Discussion : It is organized for the common man's problems. Public panel discussions are organised in Television programme on current problems such as educated unemployment, annual budget, increase in prices of things, delinking jobs from degrees.

Educational panel discussion : To provided factual and conceptual knowledge and clarification of certain theories and principles. It is used in educational institutions. Sometimes these are organised to find out the solution of certain problems. Educational panel discussions are very usefully though they are not used in most of the institutions even at higher level. Commonly conferences, seminars, symposiums and workshops are organised, which provides different types of situations for group discussion. The situation of panel discussion is usually of autocratic where as other techniques have democratic situations of group discussion.

Role of Panel Discussion

Role of Instructor: Instructor plays the most important role in the panel discussion. It is his responsibility of instructor, how, where and when panel discussion will be organized. He prepares to decide the schedule of panel discussion by him. Sometimes he has to plan rehersal of discussion.

Role of Moderator: The moderator has to do significant job in the discussion. He has to keep the discussion on theme and encourage interaction among the members. He has to summarize and highlight the discussion. He must have mastery on the theme or problem of discussion.

Role of Panelists: There are four to ten panellists in the discussion. The members of the panel sit in semi-circle before the audience. The moderator sits middle of the panalists. The panalists must have the mastery on the theme of the discussion.

Role of Audience: After the panel discussion, audience are allowed to put question and seek clarification. They can present their point of view and their experiences regarding the theme or problem. The panellists attempt to answer the questions of the audience. Sometimes the moderator also tries to answer the questions. At the end of the discussion, the moderator summarises the discussion and presents his point of view. He expresses thanks to panellists and audience.

Advantages of Discussion Technique

- It encourages social learning.
- It achieves higher cognitive and affective objectives.
- It develops the ability of problem solving and logical thinking.
- It develops the interest and right type of attitude towards the problem.
- It develops the capacity to respect others ideas and feelings and ability of tolerance.
- It provides opportunities for assimilation of the theme and its content.

Suggestions for Organizing Panel Discussion

1. *Rehearsal :* There should be rehearsal before the actual panel discussion.
2. *Mature Moderator :* The moderator should be matured person and have the full understanding of theme or problem. He should have control over the situation.

3. *Proper Seating Arrangement* : The seating arrangement for panelists and audience should be such that every one should be at equal distance and they can observe each other.

4. *Constructive Approach* : The moderator should encourages the discussion on the point which may lead to constructive aspect of the problem. He should encourage construct discussion among panelists and audience.

SYMPOSIUM TECHNIQUE

One of the techniques of higher learning. Symposium technique is also an instructional technique used to achieve higher cognitive and affective objectives. The word 'symposium' has several dictionary meanings. First of all, Plato used this term for 'good dialogue' to present the views towards god. Another meaning of the term is the intellectual recreation or enjoyment. The recent meaning of the term is a meeting of persons to discuss a problem or theme in which views are presented in a sequence. The specific aspect of a theme is presented by an expert of the theme. Thus, the symposium technique forums serves as an excellent device for informing an audience, crystallizing opinion and preparing the listeners to arrive at decision, policies, value, judgement or understanding. Its main purpose is to provide understanding to the students or listeners on theme or problem to develop specifically certain values and feelings.

Precautions for Symposium

Preparation: The moderator should prepare the speakers or see that they are prepared. They should know the rules of procedure, sequence of speaking, and way in which the forum will be conducted. They should be aware of the ideas and background of the other performers. They might benefit from a brief warm up.

Comprehensive Approach: The chairman or whosoever is responsible for preparing the agenda, should not attempt to stack the cards by omitting or ignoring vital phases of the problem as he selects or delegates his speakers. It is not good to face up to an inadvertent misinterpretation or omission. To distort or omit an important point of view deliberately is to invite disaster.

Planning Questioning Period: ***In all the forum situations th***e chairman must plan very carefully for the questioning period that follows the prepared speeches, unless he wishes to risk boredom or bedlam.

Characteristics of Symposium

- It provides broad understating of a topic or a problem.
- It provides opportunity to the listeners to take decision about the problem.
- It is used for higher classes to discuss specific themes and problems.
- It develops the sense of cooperation and adjustment.
- In it synthesis and evaluation are achieved.
- It provides different views on the subject of the symposium.

Limitations of Symposium

- The chairman has no control over the speakers who have full freedom to prepare the theme for discussion. They can present any aspect of the themes or problem.
- There is a probability of repletion because every speaker prepares theme as a whole. If different aspects of the theme are not prepared separately it creates difficulty of understanding to the listeners.
- If different aspects of theme are presented simultaneously, the listeners are not able to understand the theme correctly.

- As they are not given opportunities to seek clarification and put questions listeners remain passive in the symposium.
- The discussion and presentation of theme is not summarized at the end. As the participants take decision according to their own, only intellect persons can make use of this technique.

SEMINAR

Seminar is an instructional technique of higher learning which involve paper reaching on a theme followed by the group discussion to clarify the complex aspects of the theme. A seminar as an instructional technique generating a situation for a group to have guided interaction among themselves on a theme which is generally presented to the group by one or more members. The person who presents the theme should have studied the theme thoroughly to make selection of relevant material. The collected material is presented in the form of a paper which is circulated among the participants in advance or before the paper reading. It provides the structure of the theme, to facilitate its communication.

Objectives of Seminar

- To develop the higher cognitive abilities - analysis, synthesis and evaluation as compared to the situations involving human interaction
- To develop the ability of keen observation experience, feelings and to present them effectively.
- To develop the ability to seek clarification and defend the ideas of others effectively.
- To develop the sense of tolerance the opposite ideas of others.
- To develop the sense of co-operation with other colleagues and respect the ideas and feeling of the others.

- To develop the emotional stability among the participants of the seminar.
- To develops good manners and skills among the participants.

Roles in Seminar

Role of the Organizer: An organizer plans and prepares the whole programme of the seminar. He decides the topic or theme of the seminar and assigns different aspects of theme to different persons who play the role of speakers. The date, time and place are decided by him. He also suggests the name of convener of the seminar. He prepares total schedule of the seminar.

Role of the President: The participants propose the name of a chairman, who is well acquainted with the theme of seminar. He must know his rights and duties as chairman of a seminar. The seminar's activities are conducted by the convener. Who directs the whole programme, encourages the participants to take part in discussion, and keeps the discussion on the theme of seminar. In certain situations he also takes parts in the discussion. He provides sufficient opportunities to each participant. At the end he summarizes the discussion and presents his viewpoint on the theme. He gives thanks to the speaker, participants, guests and observers.

Role of Speakers: The organizer assigns topics to the speakers. Who study the topics thoroughly and prepare papers. Cyclostyle copies of the papers are distributed among the participants before the commencement of the seminar. So that they may also prepare themselves on the theme. It encourages discussion to last long. The speakers should be ready to defend their positions. They should have tolerance for anti-ideas or criticism of others.

Role of Participants: There are 25 to 40 participants in the seminar. The participants of the seminar should be well acquainted with the theme. They should appreciate the performances of the speakers. They should be able to seek clarification and put questions. They should place their own ideas regarding the theme on the basis of their experiences. They should address the president for seeking clarification. They should not put question directly to the speakers.

Role of Observers: Some guests and observers are also invited and allowed to observe the activities of the seminar. They should be allowed to discuss and present their observations by permission of the chairman.

Types of Seminar

One the basis of levels of organization, the seminars are of four types: (1) Mini Seminar, (2) Main Seminar, (3) National Seminar and (4) International Seminar.

Mini Seminar: A seminar organized to discuss a topic in a class is known as mini-seminar. It purposes is to train the students for organizing the seminar and play different roles. It is a stimulated situation for the students. Such seminars should be organised before the main seminar.

Main Seminar: Such seminars are organised at departmental level or institutional level on a major theme. All the students and staff members take part in main seminars. Main seminars as organized weekly or monthly in departments. Generally specific themes are selected for main seminar.

National Seminar: A national seminar is organized by an association or organization at national level. Experts are invited on the theme of the seminar. The secretary of the seminar prepares the schedule theme, time, dates, days and venue. NCERT organizes such seminar at national level, education technology, population education, trends of education, quality control of educational research in India.

International Seminar: Generally such seminars are organised by UNESCO and other international organization on very broad topic or theme such as students unrest or activism, Innovations in teacher-education and examination reform etc. A Nation can also organise such seminars on international theme.

Advantages of a Seminar

- As an instructional technique the seminar has the potential to develop several abilities among participants.
- Due to the stimulation of thinking brought about through interaction, different higher cognitive abilities like, analytical and critical thinking, synthesing and evaluating the ideas tend to be developed.
- Certain affective attributes like tolerance for other's views, openness to ideas, cooperation with others, emotional stability and respect for other's feelings may be inculcated among the participants during the course of such sessions.
- A seminar has great instructional value as it makes the instruction learner centered and provides for learning through enquiry based on the natural inquisitiveness in human beings.

Limitations of Seminar

- A seminar can not be organized on all the content of subject matter. Its theme should be such on which discussion may be held.
- Seminar technique can not be used on all levels of education but only on higher level of education.
- When a seminar is being organized, habitual speakers dominate the discussion and do not provide opportunities to others to take part in the seminar.
- During the discussion, groups are formed in two ideas- anti ideas and favourable ideas on the theme. Both try to win over the other. Therefore, the purpose of the seminar is not serves.
- Criticism made for the sake of critism. The instructional situation of such discussion is not conducive for learning.

Seminar and Workshop Difference

A seminar is a presentation on a topic covering some fact of knowledge or skill. Seminars tend to be a blend of lecture and discussion. The program can be public or private and the presentation is often organized into modules. The speaker's goal is to impart knowledge of the topic, and he or she typically uses a combination of lecture, visual aids, interaction with participants, and exercises to get the job done. Due to the emphasis on theory and the imparting of information, a seminar is typically no more than half a day (three hours).

A workshop is similar to a seminar but with a greater degree of attendee participation, interaction, and hands-on exercises, is usually a full day (six hours) where participants learn and practice the knowledge and skills that is the workshop's focus.

MODES OF TEACHING

Computer Assisted Instruction (CAI)

Computer Assisted Instruction is nothing but learning with the help of computers. It can be used to impart formal and non-formal education at all levels and also in all areas. This CAI has been developed from the principles of programmed Instruction. It is one of the types of individualized instruction. The computer assisted or aided instruction may be defined as the use of a computer as an integral part of an instruction system, the learner generally engaging in two-way interaction with the computer via terminal.

History of CAI

CAI is a natural outgrowth of the application of the principles of programmed instruction or learning. The device may enable a person to use some selected part of the stored information. A computer fulfils all these requirements. It can store the organized information; it can process the information suiting to the needs of individual learner. In short, CAI covers the entire educational system by proving itself a useful too in teaching various subjects.

Operations of CAI

CAI system has been used at all levels of education ranging from elementary school to post-graduate study and on job training in almost all subjects. Atkinson (1968) designed a programmer for teaching reading to infants. The child first must learn to identify letters. This task of identifying letters is done in three stages of the programme.

1. ***First Stage***: A Model letter appears on the projector connected with a computer, while three letters are presented on the screen. Then the recorded voice instructs the child at the letter on the projector. Different letters are shown on the projector; training is imparted to the child in identifying the letters.
2. ***Second Stage***: At this stage, the child masters the identification of single letter. During this phase the child learns to discriminate pairs of letters.
3. ***Third Stage***: During this stage, two-three letters combinations are presented on the screen. The child is asked to touch one symbol out of the two combinations which are identical.

A recorded voice asks the child to touch and say the word that would be formed by combining the letters on the side and top of the screen. Errors made by the child are automatically recorded in the computer. The child thus receives practice. The drills that various learners receive may be entirely different from each other. After masterly of simple reading skills, the child proceeds to acquire successively more complex skills. Computers have been designed to store and retrieve vast amount of information.

Modes of CAI

In the field of instructions, a computer plays a major role. In these computer assisted instructions, is interacts directly with the learners while presenting lessons. The computer delivers instructions directly to students and permits them to interact with the computer through the lessons programmed in the system. There are various instructional modes which can be facilitating by computer assisted instructions (CAI).

1. ***Tutorial Mode:*** In tutorial, information is presented in small units followed by a question. The pupils' response is analysed by the computer and appropriate feedback is given. A network of branches or pathways can be programmed to teach. The pupils are allowed to work on their own pace. The more alternative programmes available to the computers, the more adaptive the tutorial can be to individual differences.

2. ***Drill or Practice:*** In this mode, the programme leads the learner through a series of examples to develop dexterity and fluency in using the skill. All correct responses are reinforced. Only on achieving the mastery by the learner, the computer will proceed further.

3. ***Discovery Mode:*** Here, inductive approach is followed. The problems are presented and the pupil solves those problems through trial and error. It is just like laboratory learning. It aims at the deeper understanding of the results obtained from discovery. Hence, complex problems can be solved.

4. ***Gaming Mode:*** This mode may or may not be instructional, but it is recreational. Sometimes learning takes place through games. This mode is especially meant for young children.

5. ***Simulation Mode:*** Here the pupil faces scaled down approximation of real life situations. Hence, realistic practice takes place without involving any risk.

6. ***Problem Solving Mode:*** Problem solving can be readily achieved provided the typical computational capability of the computer is available and there is a typewriter and display response device with remote control of two-way communication. The students need to know

how to communicate with computer and how to solve his problem.

Advantages of CAI

(a) *Immediate Feedback :* The immediate feedback provided by interactive terminals keeps students interacting and eager to keep trying.

(b) *Active participation :* Even weaker students are obliged to participate actively. They often remain passive in lectures.

(c) *No annoyance:* The computer will wait patiently for an answer and does not express annoyance with wrong response.

(d) *Graphics facility:* Interactive graphics make it possible to sample many more illustrations that could easily be shown in a text-book.

(e) *Mathematical calculations:* Mathematical calculations can be done as readily for realistic examples as for artificially simple class that can be solved analytically.

(f) *Accurate data:* Large volumes of data can be handled with accuracy and without drudgery.

(g) *Enrichment of course:* The novel technique provides enrichment of course through added variety.

Limitations of CAI

(a) *Problem of maintenance:* The computer assisted instruction poses a great problem with regard to the effective maintenance of his learning system.

(b) *Costly:* Computer assisted instruction is very costly. The repair work or its servicing causes a serious problem to the institutions.

(c) *Non-human quality:* Computer assisted instruction may inject a non-human quality into educational programmes. This new technology may 'dehumanise' man.

Computer Managed Instructions (CMI)

In computer managed instructions, the computer gathers, stores and manages information to guide students through individualized learning experience.

At the computer is being used in administrative and management, these days, such type of computer is known as computer based learning, for example in disbursing the salaries of the teachers and other employers. Computer is not used directly in teaching-learning process, but is used as a helper in teaching-learning process. If a teacher is made free by assigning his other duties to the computer such as administrative, mangemental activities, and then he can utilize his spare time in an effective manner in the class-room.

In this way, the main function of the computer is clerical. Generally the following are the main administrative and managerial functions of the computer.

- This can prepare question papers, can evaluate them. Their scores can be analyzed for evaluation or modification purposes.
- This can collect the examination or evaluation scores.
- This can help the teachers in preparing time-table
- This can help various clerical jobs such as preparing teacher's salaries, completion of their presence records etc.

It is very clear that the computer has become an integral part of our daily routine. Computer literacy is the today's necessity. Hence, it is needed to include the computer education in secondary curriculum. On this purpose, a project class was started in 1984-85. it stands for computer literacy and studies in schools. It was started in 248 selected schools. Then later on. 2522 more schools were included in this project. Under this project, each school was provided with BCAXOROY micro-computer systems with other devices. This object has the following objectives.

- To provide detailed computer knowledge to the pupils.
- To provide knowledge to the pupils by doing themselves.
- To provide various experiences of computer education in the various fields of life.
- To remove various misconceptions regarding computers.
- To provide knowledge about computer application-according to own environment.

What is Web-Based Instruction?

Web-Based Instruction has evolved from any number of computer-based instructional methods, often referred to as Computer Assisted Instruction (CAI), Computer-aided Instruction (CAI), Computer-Managed Instruction (CMI), Internet-Based Instruction (IBI) or Web-Based Instruction (WBI), but collectively called Computer-Based Education (CBE). CBE that uses the World Wide Web as a repository for instructional information and the Internet to as Web-Based Instruction (WBI).

As McCormack and Jones (1998) wrote "It means you can use the Web as a repository students can access to retrieve any information that would be useful to them. Not only can you use the Web to help distribute information- you can also place the information in a form that goes beyond text and takes advantages of the media that will help students understand better and to which they can relate more easily". The emergence of the World Wide Web as a pipeline for learning will have a profound effect on the manner in which our students learn and we teach.

Use of Web-based Instruction

There are a number of reasons why a teacher might choose to use Web-Based Instruction, including:

- Enhancing student learning;
- Spending more time with students working in small groups or one-on-one;
- Reducing repetitive teaching tasks;
- Reducing paper flow and management, and;
- Providing improved instructional materials.

For, creating of Web-Based Instruction, McCormack and Jones (1998) suggested that one reason for doing so is because "More educators aim to use a teaching method that is effective, efficient, and enjoyable". Using Web-Based Instruction (WBI) is all of these things, but it is also pedagogically sound because it allows teachers to spend more time working with students in small groups and individually. WBI can begin to offer a variety of paths though the curriculum and offers students a self-paced learning environment, thus providing students with a sense of control over their learning. In addition, Web-Based Instruction facilitates multiple levels of instruction in one room with a single teacher. If implemented on the World Wide Web, students can have access to instructional materials at home. Because the instructional materials are stored and distributed electronically, Web-Based Instruction is also environmentally friendly, and there is not the management issues associated with paper-based instruction such as duplicating, revising, filing, and picking up after students. Students who miss school are also able to go to a Web site and find instructional materials they missed during their absence.

When used as an instructional tool, the Internet has the potential to meet the needs of a variety of students by presenting instructional materials to them in different ways, including a traditional linear form; or, with the addition of illustrations, video clips, and even sound, in such a manner that students can review or move ahead through content. Students need not follow a lock-step regimen to learning but are able to pursue learning in a self-paced manner.

Principles of Web-based Learning

- The learning experiences designed for web-based teaching must focus specific learning objectives and outcomes.
- The learner should be actively engaged and made to feel the real-life experiences through simulation.
- Keeping in mind the various learning styles of students a variety of media are made use of to develop appropriate learning environment to achieve the desired learning out-comes.
- Learning environment must include both knowledge based as well as problem-based learning, knowledge based learning involves recall, comprehension and application whereas problem-based learning focuses on higher order cognitive abilities like analysis, synthesis and evaluation.
- Learning experiences must reflect the needs and interest of the community. Provisions should be made for the visitors of the web-site to react and exchange ideas with it.

Characteristics of Web-based Learning

Quality web-based learning has the following characteristics:

- Develops the ability to derive meaning and engage in active discourse.
- Encourages the learners to collect the information they need and develop their own knowledge instead of providing tailor-made knowledge.
- Provides for the teacher and the taught to share information mutually.
- It is learner-centered and encourages active participation and knowledge-construction.
- Fosters the higher order cognitive abilities like analysis, synthesis and evaluation.

- Allow for group learning too, encourages collaboration and cooperation among the group members to collect and share the needed information.
- Focuses on real-world events and problem-solving

Merits of Web-Based Learning

Web based learning has the following advantages.

- Moves from knowledge transmission to learner controlled systems.
- Provides for reciprocal teaching.
- Is learner centered. Self paced learning is possible in this methods
- Encourages active participation, knowledge constructions
- Based on higher level thinking skills-analysis, synthesis and evaluation
- Promotes active learning
- Allows group collaboration and cooperative learning.
- Provides multiple levels of interaction
- Focuses on real-world, problem solving.
- More and recent information related to topic can be accessed and delivered.
- Updated information is available in the web sites.
- More information will be gathered in short duration of time. So energy and time will be saved.
- Abstract concepts can be easily explained with the help of animation and graphics.
- It can be used for increasing course delivery for a large number of clients at a particular point of time.
- Learners on the job are facilitated own time access and interaction.
- Instructional materials are already instructionally designed for wider use.

- Web based instruction will be more effective at higher education and research level.

Limitations of Web Based Learning

The web based learning has the following limitations:

- Since course materials are instructionally pre-designed, it hardly provides for individual variation and further revision.
- If not properly designed and navigated, one may manually turn pages, which is demotivating to many.
- Access to internet may be limited.
- Information may not be available related to all topics.
- Information may not be available in all languages or regional languages.
- There is no mechanism available to establish standards for internet materials, instructional design, and quality of interaction.
- It is difficult to alter the varying reaching styles of teachers and varying learning styles of learners.

It need to be designed, developed, and implemented very carefully otherwise its credibility would be at stake.

5.

Teaching Skills

Microteaching

A teacher makes use of number of methods and techniques to bring about effective learning. The techniques include, motivating the students, explaining, questioning, writing on the blackboard, using teaching aids and so on. The teacher could also make use of nonverbal behaviours such as smiling, nodding and gesturing. These groups of activities are called skills. A teaching skill is a group of teaching acts/behaviours intended to facilitate pupils' learning directly or indirectly. If the teacher trainees are conscious and aware of teaching skills, they will be able to concentrate on each of these skills and gain masterly over the skill. Microteaching introduces the teacher trainee to a wide range of teaching skills and allows the teacher trainee to practice each skill one at a time until he or she becomes proficient in the skill. Later on, the teacher trainee will be able to link many such skills to achieve the desirable outcome.

Definitions

Microteaching has been defined in many ways likes:

- Microteaching as a scaled down teaching encounter in class size and class time. *– Allen D.W. (1966)*
- Micro teacher as a teacher training procedure which reduced the teaching situation to a simpler and more controlled encounter achieved by limiting the practice of teaching to a specific skill and reducing teaching time and class size. *– Clift et al., (1976)*
- Microteaching as a system of controlled practice, that makes it possible to concentrate on specific teaching

behavior and to practice teaching under controlled conditions.

—*Allen Eve (1968)*

- The most important point in microteaching is that teaching is practiced in terms of definable, observable, measurable and controllable teaching skills.

—*Passi B.K.*

From the above stated definitions a more comprehensive definition of microteaching can be stated as follows. Microteaching is a teacher training technique where the complexities of the normal classroom teaching are reduced by:

- Practicing one teaching skill at a time
- Limiting the content to a single concept
- Reducing the class size to 5 to 7 and
- Reducing the duration of the lesson to 5 to 7 minutes.

Characteristics of Microteaching

- Microteaching is a teacher training techniques and not a teaching method.
- Microteaching is real teaching, though the teaching situation is simulated.
- In microteaching the teacher trainee practices one specific teaching skill at a time, till he/she attains masterly over the skill.
- Microteaching is a scaled down teaching encounter in class size (5-7 students), content (one concept) and class time (5-7 minutes).
- Microteaching operates on predicated model: Plan, Teach, Feedback, Re-Plan, Re-teach, Re-feedback, Re-Plan etc.
- Microteaching allows for increased control of practice by providing feedback to the teacher trainee.
- Microteaching is not a substitute, but a supplement to the teacher-training programme.

Use of Microteaching

Microteaching technique enhances the effectiveness of the teacher training programmes in the following ways.

- Microteaching helps in reducing the complexities of the normal classroom teaching. This helps the teacher trainees gain more confidence in real teaching.
- Microteaching creates among the teacher-trainees an awareness of the various skills of which teaching is composed of.
- Microteaching helps in systematic and objective analysis of the pattern of classroom communication through specific observation schedule.
- Microteaching simulates the classroom scene and gives the teacher trainee an experience of real teaching.
- Feedback enables the teacher-trainees to consciously concentrate on specific behaviour modification.
- As microteaching focuses on the modification of behavior and improvement of interaction process involved in teaching learning process, the teacher trainees can handle classes more effectively in real teaching.
- In microteaching the complex task of teaching is looked upon as a set of simpler skills comprising specific classroom behaviour. This helps the teacher trainees in better understanding of the meaning and concept of the term 'teaching'.
- Objectives can be defined more easily and more reliable measures of change in teacher behavior can be thought of using behaviorally defined skills.

Teaching Skills

Microteaching technique rests upon the analytical approach to teaching. Analytical approach assumes that the complex task of teaching can be analysed into limited, but well defined components called 'teaching skills'. Each of these teaching skills can be taught, practiced, evaluated, predicted, controlled and understood.

Teaching skills have been defined differently by different authors. Gagne (1968) defined the teaching skills "as specific instructional activities and procedures that a teacher may use in his classroom". According to McIntyre and White "technical skill is a set of related teaching behaviours which in specified types of classroom instruction situations tend to facilitate the achievement of specified types of classroom interaction situations tend to facilitate the achievement of specified type of objectives". All these definitions specify that a teaching skill is a group of teaching acts/behaviours intended to facilitate pupils' learning activity directly or indirectly.

Characteristics of Teaching Skills

Teaching skills have three basic components, viz, perception, cognition and action.

Teaching skills have three basic dimensions: a) non-verbal behaviour, b) openness and c)nature of moves in teaching to which the skill belongs.

Types of Teaching Skills

Attempts have been made to list teaching skills that could be developed among the student-teachings. A large number of skills have been identified. However, there is no uniformity in the number and categories of teaching skills. Fourteen teaching skills have been listed in Stanford University (Allen and Rayan, 1969) whereas Singh L.C.(1979) identified twenty two general teaching skills. Later on Menon et al (1983) have suggested a list of seventy four skills.

The important skills pertaining to the areas of motivation, presentation, questioning and recapitulation have been chosen and listed below.

- Set induction
- Explanation

- Questioning
- Stimulus variation
- Reinforcement
- Closure
- Blackboard work

Skill of Set Induction (skill of motivation)

This is a pre-instructional technique. The teacher, before introducing a lesson has to prepare the minds of the students to receive new knowledge. For effective learning, the teacher has to ensure students' willingness to learn. The learning becomes more meaningful when the new knowledge is integrated with the previous knowledge. Hence the teacher should set a stage for enabling the students to recall the previous knowledge and relate it with the new experience. The following behaviours are essential for set induction.

- Establishing a cognitive and affective rapport with the pupils.
- Recalling and integrating previous knowledge with new knowledge.
- Maintaining continuity and logical links
- Arousing and maintaining the student interest.

The main components of the skill are:

- Arrest attention
- Focus attention on the topic
- Introduce an element of interest
- Arouse the curiosity

Set Induction: Components and Their Description

S.No.	*Components*	*Description of Behaviour*
1	Arrest attention	• Use of voice gesture and eye contact. • Use of audiovisual aids • Changing the pattern of teacher-pupil interaction.

S.No.	Components	Description of Behaviour
2	Focus attention on the topic	• Test the previous knowledge relevant for learning the new topic. • Can also use knowledge acquired from various source like classroom, books, friends etc. • Maintain logical continuity. • Integrate the old knowledge with the new knowledge.
3	Introduce an element of interest	• Using teaching aids like flash card, charts, models etc. • Using other devices like analogies, story telling, brief history of any subject etc. • Bringing out the significance of the new lesson
4	Arouse the curiosity	• Creating a suitable learning situation Posing an intriguing problem.

Skill of Explanation

A teacher is said to be explaining when he is describing 'how', 'why' and sometimes 'what' of a concept, phenomenon, event, action or condition. It can be described as an activity to bring about an understanding in the learning about a concept, principle. etc. While explaining the teacher gives.

- Causes for some phenomena, event or action
- Reason for some phenomena, event or action
- Steps involved in arriving at a result or
- Various events that have resulted in phenomena

Explaining bridges the gap in understanding the new knowledge by relating it to the past experience. Thus explaining depends upon the type of the past experience, the type of the new knowledge and the type of the relationship between them. Explanations can be made more effective by using simple and clear language for clarity, examples and illustration materials for better understanding and appropriate link words for relating the concepts be given.

Components and Description of Skill of Explanation

S.No.	*Components*	*Description of Behaviour*
1.	Beginning statement	• Gaining attention/arousing interest Today we are going to derive/ discuss/describe
2.	Clarity	• State concepts clearly • Define new terms and concepts; use simple language, maintain logical sequence. • Use suitable examples and illustration. • Voice modulation to emphasis. • Develop the explanation from: Known to unknown. Examples to rule.
3.	Fluency	Use simple language/easy flow of ideas/use appropriate vocabulary
4.	Use of link words	• Use linking words and phrases. Example : therefore, similarly, that is, since, that is why, because, in order to, hence ... etc.
5.	Planned repetition	• Provide summaries to refocus attention • Deliberately repeat some important concepts or points.
6.	Stimulating questions	• Check the understanding by questioning. • Stimulate and channelise the students thinking by thought provoking questions like how, why type.
7.	Concluding statement	• Consolidate the ideas by summarizing • Conclude the explanation by statements like 'Thus we have proved/so far we discuss' etc.

Skill of Stimulus Variation

It is very important for a teacher to ensure and sustain pupil's attention. For this purpose the teacher uses some gestures, body movements, makes certain verbal statements etc. all these behaviours are related to stimulus variation. The skill of stimulus variation can be defined as deliberate change in the attention drawing behaviours of the teacher in order to secure and sustain pupil's attention towards the lesson.

Components and Description of Skill of Stimulus Variation

S.No.	*Components*	*Description of Behaviour*
1	Teacher movement	• Movement of the teacher from one spot to another with a specific purpose. Eg. Moves to the blackboard to write something on the board. Moves towards the back of the classroom to check what the students are doing. • Purposeful movement of the teacher from one spot to another
2	Teacher gesture	• Gestures, body movements and facial expressions to direct attention, to emphasize importance, to explain emotions, to indicate size, shapes etc. • Nonverbal cues like body movements, facial expressions etc.
3	Change in sensory focus	• Focusing pupils attention on particular point or concept by using (1) verbal statement like 'look at the blackboard', 'see the figure in the chart' etc. (2) gestures and (3) both verbal statements and non-verbal cues. • Making use of the different senses like hearing, seeing, touching and so on.
4	Change in speech pattern	• Voice modulation to pay special attention to a particular point. • Variation in time, pitch, speed of voice

S.No.	*Components*	*Description of Behaviour*
5	Physical pupil pattern	• Variation in physical involvement of the students • Eg: student moves towards the blackboard to work out a problem. Student holds the chart.
6	Verbal pupil pattern	• Involvement of the students through verbal communication style as: (1) teacher to group (2)teacher to student (3) student to student • Example: asking questions, discussion etc.

Skill of Reinforcement

Reinforcement is strengthening the connection between a stimulus and a response. There are two types of reinforcements i.e. positive reinforcement and negative reinforcement. Positive reinforcement provide pleasant experience or a feeling of satisfaction which contributes towards strengthening of desirable responses or behaviours. The negative reinforcement results in unpleasant experiences, which help in weakening the occurrence of undesirable responses or behaviours.

The skill of reinforcement can increase the students involvement in learning in a number of ways. The skill is used when the teacher reinforces correct responses with a smile, when the teacher praises a good response or encourages a slow learner. Such positive reinforces strengthen desirable responses whereas negative reinforces such as scolding, punishing the students, sarcastic remarks etc. weaken the undesirable response. However, the use of more and more positive reinforcers maximizes pupils' involvement of learning rather than the use of negative reinforcers. Therefore, the skills of reinforcement involve the teacher to use more and more positive reinforcers and to decrease the use of negative reinforcers so that the pupils' participation is maximized.

Components and Description of Skill of Reinforcement

S.No.	Components	Description of Behaviour
1.	Positive verbal reinforcement	Comments like 'good', 'very good', 'excellent' etc
2.	Positive gestures	Facial expression; example; 'smile'
3.	Proximity	Teacher moving towards the responding student
4.	Token reinforcement	merit card
5.	Activity reinforcement	Giving a task, the student likes to perform
6.	Negative verbal	Comments like 'nonsense'
7.	Negative gesture	Facial expression like 'frowning'

Skill of Probing Questions

Questioning skill is an important skill to be developed by any teacher. It is all the more important for all teacher as questioning stimulates the thinking of the students and gets the concepts clarified and hence has significant contribution to teaching and learning for all subjects. Probing is going deep into the pupils' responses by asking a number of questions about what they already know and to lead them to the correct response or to remove any ambiguity or misconception, which has led to such responses. Probing is to be done where there is no response, or incorrect response, or partially right response.

Components and Description of Skill of Probing Questions

S.No.	Components	Description of Behaviour
1	Prompting	This technique is going deep into the pupil's initial response. This technique is employed when the student gives no response to the correct response with a series of hints or prompts through step-by-step questioning process. Giving hints or clues to lead the student from no response or wrong response to correct response.

S.No.	Components	Description of Behaviour
2	Seeking further information	This technique involves leading a pupil from partially correct or incomplete response to the correct response through questioning. Questions that lead the students from partially correct incomplete response to correct answer.
3	Refocusing	This technique is employed when the student gives completely correct response. Refocusing through questioning helps the pupils to view the correct response from a different viewpoint. Questions that help the student to view his correct response in a broader perspective.
4	Redirection	Directing the same questions to other pupils when there is a wrong response, incomplete response, partially right response, or while prompting or while seeking further information and so on.
5	Increasing critical awareness	It involves putting questions such as 'how' and 'why' to increase the critical awareness of the pupils about the correct response. Thus this technique is followed when the students give correct response.

Skill of Blackboard Writing

Blackboard is an important visual aid used by teachers for effective teaching. A teacher makes extensive use of blackboard in his or her daily classroom teaching for working our problems, deriving formulae, proving theorems, drawing figures, constructing geometrical figures and so on. Every teacher should be proficient in the skill of using blackboard. Good blackboard writing leads to the following:

- Clarity in the understanding of concepts

- Reinforcement of the idea which is being verbally presented.
- Conveying a holistic picture of the content.
- Adding variety to the lesson and drawing attention of the pupils to the key concepts.

Components and Description of Skill of Blackboard Writing

S.No.	*Components*	*Description of Behaviour*
1.	Legibility in hand writing	• Distinct letters • Adequate spacing between letters and words • Adequate size for the letters • Different sizes for capital and small letters • Uniform size for all capital letters • Uniform size for all small letters
2.	Neatness in blackboard work	• Straightness of lines • Adequate spacing between the lines • Avoiding overwriting • Focusing the relevant matter
3.	Appropriateness of blackboard work	• Continuity in the ideas • Brevity and simplicity • Drawing attention and focusing

Skill of Closure

It is an important skill to achieve closure at the end of the lesson.

Components and Description of Skill of Closure

S.No.	*Components*	*Description of Behaviour*
1.	Consolidation of major points	• Synthesizing of the learning points into a meaningful whole. • Reviewing the content in a broader perspective.

S.No.	*Components*	*Description of Behaviour*
		• Use of number of mediums– Example: Blackboard Summary, Questions, A.V.Aids. etc.,
2	Application of present knowledge in various new situations	• Application in problem solving • Use of any medium. Examples: Questioning-oral or written, diagrams, charts, map etc.
3	Linking past knowledge with present knowledge	• Make the pupils review the past knowledge in the light of the present knowledge. • Use of a variety of approaches-questioning, summary statements, using nonverbal media like blackboard, charts etc.
4	Linking present knowledge with future learning	• Appropriate assignments related to the present knowledge.

INTEGRATION OF TEACHING SKILLS / LINK LESSON

There is little doubt that the effectiveness of microteaching is diminished if its is made into an isolated event. In most of the teacher training colleges, micro teaching is used in one or all the following ways.

- As a preparation of practice teaching.
- As a remedy for teacher trainees whose classroom techniques have been found to be lacking in some way.
- As an aid to translate educational theory to practical classroom methods.
- As a way of prompting experienced teachers to evaluate their classroom skills.

However no amount of experience in any one skill can promise a good lesson. It is the integration of two or more selected microteaching skills which forms a macro lesson that is of a full 40 or 45 minutes period. The transition form a micro teaching session to a macro teaching session which is done by taking a few selected skills with more content than in a micro lesson through link practice. A link lesson gives a student trainee taste of a real class without panic and uncertainly associated with a macro lesson. Thus a full unit can be chosen for link practice. The unit is then divided into several smaller portions and with a few selected micro skills, a link lesson can be framed.

This gives an opportunity to use even those skills which may not have been practiced before. This lesson can be demonstrated to a group of teacher trainees who can then practice continuously with no break in the subject matter. Integration of teaching skills is characterized by:

- The appropriates of the use of skills integrated.
- Adaptability to other situations.
- Proper sequencing of the skills
- Optimum portions of each skill in teaching.
- Co-ordination of different elements involved in teaching.

EVALUATION OF TEACHING SKILLS

All assessment and evaluation techniques contain implicit assumptions about the characteristics that constitute quality teaching. These assumptions should be made explicit and indeed should become part of the evaluation process itself in a manner which recognizes instructors' rights to be evaluated within the context of their own teaching philosophies and goals. First and foremost then, "teaching is not right or wrong, good or bad, effective or ineffective in any absolute, fixed or determined sense." Instructors emphasize different domains of learning (affective, cognitive, psychomotor, etc.) and employ different theories of education and teaching methodologies (anti-racist, constructivist, critical, feminist, humanistic, etc.). They encourage learning in different sites (classrooms, field locations, laboratories, seminar rooms, studios, virtual classrooms, etc.). They use different instructional strategies and formats (using case studies, coaching, demonstrating, facilitating discussions, lecturing, problem based learning, online delivery, etc.), and they do this while recognizing that students have diverse backgrounds and levels of preparedness. In one situation, instructors may see their role as transmitting factual information, and in another as facilitating discussion and promoting critical thinking.

As variable and diverse as quality teaching might be, generalizations may nevertheless be made about its basic characteristics as described in the accompanying text box. The criteria for evaluating teaching vary between disciplines and within disciplines, and should take into consideration the level of the course, the instructor's objectives and style, and the teaching methodology employed. Nonetheless, the primary criterion must be improved student learning. Research indicates that students, faculty and administrators alike agree that ***quality teaching***:

- establishes a positive learning environment;
- motivates student engagement;
- provides appropriate challenges;
- is responsive to students' learning needs; and
- is fair in evaluating their learning.

Concretely, indicators of quality teaching can include:

- effective choice of materials;
- organization of subject matter and course;
- effective communication skills;
- knowledge of and enthusiasm for the subject matter and teaching;
- availability to students; and
- responsiveness to student concerns and opinions.

Some characteristics are more easily measured than others. Furthermore, since instructors are individuals and teaching styles are personal, it is all the more important to recognize that not everyone will display the same patterns and strengths.

Assessment of Teaching

Formative Evaluation: Evaluation that is used for the purpose of self-improvement is defined as "formative evaluation". The instructor collects student and peer perceptions of teaching effectiveness solely for the purposes of modifying and enhancing teaching strategies.

Formative assessment of teaching can be carried out at many points during an instructional period, in the classroom or virtual environment, to compare the perceptions of the instructor with those of the students, and to identify gaps between what has been taught and what students have learned. The purpose of assessment is for instructors to find out what changes they might make in teaching methods or style, course organization or content, evaluation and grading procedures, etc., in order to improve student learning. Assessment is initiated by the instructor and information and feedback can be solicited from many sources (for example, self, students, colleagues, consultants) using a variety of instruments (surveys, on-line forms, etc.). The data gathered are seen only by the instructor and, if desired, a consultant, and form the basis for ongoing improvement and development.

Summative Evaluation: Evaluation for the purpose of making personnel decisions and for enhancing teaching effectiveness is defined as "summative evaluation". Administrators and departmental voting faculty evaluate data from students, peers, and the instructor in order to make informed decisions regarding reappointment, promotion and tenure, for post tenure review of faculty, teaching awards or for consideration of merit pay increases.

Summative evaluation, by contrast, is usually conducted at the end of a particular course or at specific points in an instructor's career. The purpose is to form a judgment about the effectiveness of a course and/or an instructor. The judgment may be used for tenure and promotion decisions, to reward success in the form of teaching awards or merit pay, or to enable departments to make informed decisions about changes to individual courses, the curriculum or teaching assignments. At most universities, summative evaluation includes the results of teaching evaluations regularly scheduled at the end of academic terms. However, to ensure that summative evaluation is both comprehensive and representative, it should include a variety of evaluation strategies, among them:

- letters from individual students commenting on the effectiveness of the instructor's teaching, the quality of the learning experience, and the impact of both on their academic progress;
- assessments by peers based on classroom visits;
- samples and critical reviews of contributions to course and curriculum development, as well as of contributions to scholarship on teaching; and
- evidence of exceptional achievements and contributions to teaching in the form of awards, and committee work.

Peer Evaluation: For reviews of teaching, the peer reviewers may be colleagues of any rank mutually agreed upon by the faculty member and the department head or academic administrator, pending resolution by the Dean if there is disagreement. The peer reviewers may be selected from inside or outside the department. In small departments or in highly specialized disciplines, it may be difficult to find colleagues who can provide the required insights within the same department.

Conclusion

The microteaching sessions provide adequate opportunities for the teacher-trainees to equip themselves with the teaching skills necessary to become effective teachers.

6.

E-Learning

Definition of e-learning

E-learning refers to the use of information and communications technology (ICT) to enhance and/or support learning in tertiary education. It covers a wide range of systems, from students using e-mail and accessing course work on line while following a course on campus to programmes offered entirely online.

E-learning can be divided into several types. In all cases, a campus-based institution is offering the courses, but using e-learning tied to the Internet or other online network to a different extent.

Web-supplemented courses focus on classroom-based teaching but include elements such as putting a course outline and lecture notes on line, use of e-mail and links to online resources.

Web-dependent courses require students to use the Internet for key elements of the programme such as online discussions, assessment, or online project/collaborative work, but without significant reduction in classroom time.

In ***mixed mode*** courses, the e-learning element begins to ***replace*** classroom time. Online discussions, assessment, or project/collaborative work replace some face-to-face teaching and learning. But significant campus attendance remains part of the mix.

And when courses are offered ***fully online***, students can follow courses offered by a university in one city from another town, country or time zone.

Scopes of e-learning

E-learning is commonly referred to the intentional use of networked information and communications technology in teaching and learning. A number of other terms are also used to describe this mode of teaching and learning. They include ***online learning, virtual learning, distributed learning, network*** and ***web based learning***. Fundamentally, they all refer to educational processes that utilize information and communications technology to mediate asynchronous as well as synchronous learning and teaching activities. On closer scrutiny, however, it will be clear that these labels refer to slightly different educational processes and as such they cannot be used synonymously with the term ***e-learning***.

The term e-learning comprises a lot more than ***online learning, virtual learning, distributed learning, networked*** or ***web-based learning***. As the letter "e" in e-learning stands for the word "electronic", e-learning would incorporate all educational activities that are carried out by individuals or groups working online or offline, and synchronously or asynchronously via networked or standalone computers and other electronic devices. These various types or modalities of e-learning activity are represented in the following Table.

Individualized self-paced e-learning *online*	Individualized self-paced e-learning *offline*
Group-based e-learning *synchronously*	Group-based e-learning *asynchronously*

Individualized self-paced e-learning online refers to situations where an individual learner is accessing learning resources such as a database or course content online via an Intranet or the Internet. A typical example of this is a learner studying alone or conducting some research on the Internet or a local network.

Individualized self-paced e-learning offline refers to situations where an individual learner is using learning resources such as a database or a computer-assisted learning package offline (i.e., while not connected to an Intranet or the Internet). An example of this is a learner working alone off a hard drive, a CD or DVD. ***Group-based e-learning synchronously*** refers to situations where groups of learners are working together in real time via an Intranet or the Internet. It may include text-based conferencing, and one or two-way audio and videoconferencing. Examples of this include learners engaged in a real-time chat or an audio-videoconference.

Group-based e-learning asynchronously refers to situations where groups of learners are working over an Intranet or the Internet where exchanges among participants occur with a time delay (i.e., not in real time). Typical examples of this kind of activity include on-line discussions via electronic mailing lists and text-based conferencing within learning managements systems.

E-learning and Traditional Learning

"It is not expected that e-learning will replace traditional forms. According to E. Masie in "The real truth about e-learning's future," in a few years "there will not be a division between e-learning and traditional learning, as learning will naturally evolve to utilize technological progress to improve learning efficiency". Most academic institutions and organizations are incorporating blended learning and not just e-learning.

This is the use of more than one strategy or delivery system for learning. As learners, we naturally learn through a variety of methods; we talk to colleagues outside of the classroom, read a book, discuss with peers, take an online class etc. E-learning has the power to enormously enrich the learning experience through the use of interactivity and multiple media, both of which are shown by education theory to greatly enhance learning effectiveness.

How is e-learning different?

Using the e-learning differs from traditional training and slide presentation in three main ways:

- An e-learning course is delivered on a computer giving learners the flexibility to take the course from the workstation on their desk or from a laptop and cellular modem at the beach.
- An e-learning application is delivered on demand rather than on a specific schedule, so learners can take the course at their own pace.
- Learners' lead-learners create their own learning experiences, with the help of the online materials you have created. Learners select which part of the material to study and in which order.

Types of E-Learning

There are a few of the most common types of e-Learning. They are as given below :

- Technology Based Learning (TBL)
- Web Based Training (WBT)
- Computer Based Training (CBT)
- Synchronous and Asynchronous e-learning

These are a few of the most common types of e-learning.

(a) ***Technology-Based Learning (TBL):*** The phrase, interchangeable with e-learning, technology-based learning includes deployment of methods that use recent technological developments such as computer-mediated communication, videoconferencing, multimedia, groupware, video on demand, desktop publishing, intelligent tutoring system, virtual reality just to name a few.

(b) ***Web-Based Training (WBT) :*** Generally web-based learning, e-learning uses streaming media, text, and graphics to develop exciting learning environment that is deployed right on the user via the internet. It is a great way to e learning for the large group of people scattered across the globe, but it can present the same deployment challenge that the audience encounters in dial-up connecting.

(c) ***Computer-Based Training (CBT)*** : This is great alternative to WBT for graphic or audio rich e-learning, computer e-learning, deployed via CD-ROM, which elements the streaming issues that can be associated with WBT.

(d) ***Synchronous and Asynchronous e-learning*** : With synchronous e-learning, learning and teaching takes place at the same time while the trainer and learners are physically separated from each other.

Examples of synchronous learning are as follows:

- Internet telephony
- Web conferencing
- Online lectures
- Distance learning via-interactive satellite
- Audio/video conferencing

Asynchronous e-learning means that the user can take the training indent of any schedule. At Resource Bridge it refers to this as "wherever they are whenever they need it," asynchronous e-learning does not need a facilitator or instructor, and is one of the more popular e learning deployment methods.

Examples of asynchronous e learning are the following:

- Self-paced courses taken via internet on CD-ROM
- Stored audio/video level presentations or seminars.

ATTRIBUTES AND BENEFITS OF E-LEARNING

Attributes

- Shorter learning time, often shorter.
- Adapts to learner needs (i.e., learning mastering is fixed but individual learning times may vary)

- Actively involves learner; frequent activity
- Ensures learning.
- Generate positive learner attitudes (when done well learners often rate e-learning activities as preferable to alternatives.)
- Provides consistent quality.
- Allows instant, worldwide updates.
- Is available 24/7/365.
- Is patient and treats all learners objectively and fairly.
- Is highly amenable to systematic improvement.
- Saves money through low cost delivery (no or minimal mized travel; fewer or no instruction; automated administration; no classrooms, supplies, whiteboard, etc.)
- Allows option for more in-depth study or review whenever needed.

Roles of Libraries in e-learning

Libraries are considered to be the heart of education with tuitions. These play a very important role in the teaching and learning environment of information society. The information needs and urgency in acquiring the needed information has made libraries to change rapidly. In order to achieve this end, the libraries use new information and communication technologies. The information communication and networking technologies have made considerable impact on traditional libraries and information centers.

In fact, technology is changing the very nature of libraries. It is exerting a major influence on the strategic direction if libraries in the society wherein the user want instant access to digitizing of documents and their storage in multimedia management systems accessible through browsers. Digital and virtual libraries, which play an important role in e learning, are fast emerging as an integration of varied technologies like hardware technology, software technology, networking, web technology etc. the internet has significantly transformed the very concept of a library. The availability of massive amounts of information on the internet requires expertise for improving the quality of searches and for constructing and maintaining database and WWW-based information services meant for end users so as to satisfy their educational and information needs. With the growing importance of rich media content in higher learning, libraries throughout the world are facing a significant challenge in meeting increasingly mobile demands of users to access these learning resources.

Suggestions to Make e-learning Possible in India

The following are some of the suggestions to make e-learning possible in India.

- Encourage all the universities to have networking among themselves by providing funds generously.
- Minimize the cost of computers and motivate the learners to purchase computers by offering loans with minimum interest.
- As Internet functioning needs the use of telephone, telephony should be technologically improved and the government should make all the local calls free, thereby Internet accessing will become cheaper.
- Internet facilities should be provided to the rural areas and computer literacy program needs to be conducted in rural areas.
- Make the knowledge of computer compulsory for all types of recruitments.
- Develop the habit of reading through computer monitors.

Advantages of e-learning

There are a number of benefits to tertiary learning online that are unique to the medium. Some of which are extracted here.

- *Any time*: A participant can access the learning programme at any time that is convenient - not just during the specific 1-3-hour period that is set for a conventional course. The episodes can be quick snatches at odd times or long late-night sessions. Cross-time-zone communication, difficult to arrange in real time, is as easy as talking to someone across town when using the Internet.
- *Any place:* The participants do not have to meet. That means they can be anywhere. International sharing is feasible. Individuals can log on at work, home, the library, in a community learning center or from their hotel when traveling.
- *Asynchronous interaction:* Unlike face-to-face or telephone conversations, electronic mail does not require participants to respond immediately. As a result, interactions can be more succinct and to-the-point, discussion can stay more on-track, and people can get a chance to craft their responses. This can lead to more thoughtful and creative conversations.
- *Group collaboration:* Electronic messaging creates new opportunities for groups to work together; creating shared electronic conversations that can be thoughtful and more permanent than voice conversations. Sometimes aided by on-line moderators, these net seminars can be powerful for learning and problem solving.
- *New educational approaches:* Many new options and learning strategies become economically feasible through online courses. For instance, the technology makes it feasible to utilize faculty anywhere in the world and to put together faculty teams that include master teachers, researchers, scientists, and experienced professional developers. Online courses also can provide unique opportunities for teachers to share innovations in their own work with the

immediate support of electronic groups and expert faculty.

- *Integration of computers:* The online learner has access to a computer, so computer applications can be used without excluding some participants. This means, for instance, that a mathematical model implemented in a spreadsheet can easily be incorporated into a lesson and downloaded so all participants can run, explore, and refine the model and then share their findings and improvements.

Advantages to the Learner

Along with the increased retention, reduced learning time, and other aforementioned benefits to students, particular advantages of e-learning include:

- *On-demand availability* enables students to complete training conveniently at off-hours or from home.
- *Self-pacing* for slow or quick learners reduces stress and increases satisfaction.
- *Interactivity* engages users, pushing them rather than pulling them through training.
- *Confidence* that refresher or quick reference materials are available reduces burden of responsibility of mastery.

Disadvantages to the Learner

The ways in which e-learning may not excel over other training include:

- *Technology issues* of the learners are most commonly techno phobia and unavailability of required technologies.
- *Portability* of training has become strength of e-learning with the proliferation of network linking points, notebook computers, PDAs, and mobile phones, but still it does not rival that of printed workbooks or reference material.

- ***Reduced*** social and cultural interaction can be a drawback. The impersonality, suppression of communication mechanisms such as body language, and elimination of peer-to-peer learning that are part of this potential disadvantage are lessening with advances in communications technologies.

Disadvantages to the Trainer or Organization

E-learning is not, however, the be all and end all to every training need. It does have limitations, among them:

- ***Up-front investment*** required of an e-learning solution is larger due to development costs. Budgets and cash flows will need to be negotiated.
- ***Technology issues*** that play a factor include whether the existing technology infrastructure can accomplish the training goals, whether additional tech expenditures can be justified, and whether compatibility of all software and hardware can be achieved.
- ***Inappropriate content*** for e-learning may exist according to some experts, though are limited in number. Even the acquisition of skills that involve complex physical/ motor or emotional components (for example, juggling or mediation) can be augmented with e-learning.
- ***Cultural acceptance*** is an issue in organizations where student demographics and psychographics may predispose them against using computers at all, let alone for e-learning.

7.

Mobile Learning

Introduction

Today the more and more rapid development of the ICT contributes to the increasing abilities of the mobile devices (cell phones, smart phones, PDAs, laptops) and wireless communications, which are the main parts of the mobile learning. On the other hand for the implementation of mobile learning it is necessary to use a corresponding system for the management of such type of education.

Mobile technology has become fairly ubiquitous in the last few years. Wireless developments in e-learning services focus on themes such as the integration of data and voice functionality in a single device, concepts of digital collaboration (blending instructor-led classroom training with elearning), wireless access to data applications, the transmission of learning modules and synchronous (communication in real-time) and asynchronous learning modes. In all of these, it is irrelevant whether a mobile phone with internet access or a handheld data device with phone capability is meant.

Definition of M-Learning

M-learning is a natural extension to conventional e-learning practice through which mobile technology allows a greater degree of access to learning resources. Currently, most e-learning experiences are based on learners accessing resources through fixed nodes such as desktop PCs, to which access is generally restricted by either location, time of day or both. Mobile learning is defined as "the provision of education and training on mobile devices: Personal Digital Assistants (PDAs), palmtops and handhelds and on smart phones and mobile phones."

This definition reflects the tension in the field of mobile learning between functionality and mobility. The devices available may be assembled on a continuum running from the most functional to the most mobile. Because the focus in mobile learning is on mobility this presentation limits the range of mobile learning limits the range of the field to the devices listed, to the exclusion of laptop computers.

M-learning Vs. e-learning

Over the past decade we have become familiar with the term e-learning and now m-learning is emerging. Comprehension definition of Urdan and Weggen (2000) provides a sufficient basis to distinguish between m-learning and e-learning: the term e-learning covers a wide set of applications and processes, including computer-based learning, web-based learning, virtual classrooms and digital collaboration. We define e-learning as the delivery of content via all electronic media, including the Internet, Intranets, Extranets, satellite broadcast, audio/video tape, interactive TV, and CD-ROM. Yet, e-learning is defined more narrowly than distance learning, which would include text-based learning and courses conducted via written correspondence.

m-learning is a subset of e-learning. E-learning is the macro concept that includes online and mobile learning environments. In this regard the following simple definition of Quin (2001) is very useful: 'M-learning is e-learning through mobile computational devices: Palms, windows CE machines, even your digital cell phone.'

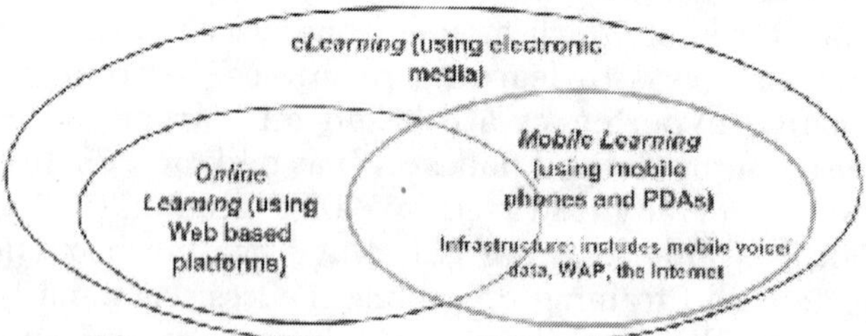

Parameters for M-Learning

The mobile revolution is finally here in the form of m-learning, which is a natural extension of e-learning. In a span of five years, Mobile learning has made an exponential leap from theory explored by academicians to a real contribution to learning. There are five basic parameters for production and development of m-learning and they are:

- ***Portable:*** If you are using a mobile phone, then it's easier to carry it along with you everywhere including the restroom. This makes information access through this platform easy and fast.
- ***Social Interaction:*** The data can be sent to your friends, colleagues and others via short massages. You can exchange data with other people and gain considerable knowledge.
- ***Sensitive to the context:*** This has capability of gathering data unique to the current location, environment, and time. This includes both types of data – real and simulated.
- ***Connectivity:*** Connectivity plays an extremely important role and is the backbone of the m-learning. With the help of a strong connectivity network, one can connect to data collection devices, other mobile phones, and to a common network.
- ***Customized:*** The most unique capability is to be able to offer customized learning information.

Types of Mobile Devices

The main types of mobile devices used in the education process are:

- ***Notebook computers.*** From one hand they have such abilities as desktop personal computer; from the other hand they have small sizes and support wireless communications. Their prices are still high.

- *Tablet PC.* These are one of the newest mobile devices. They also have full range of abilities as personal computers. Some of them haven't keyboard but have software to recognise handwritten text. It is relatively expensive.
- *Personal Digital Assistant (PDA).* They have small sizes and significant processor power. New models support more than 65000 colors, recognise handwritten text and can play different types of multimedia files. The main operating systems used are Palm and Microsoft Pocket PC.
- *Cellular phones.* The low class devices mainly can be used for voice communication and sending and receiving of text messages (SMS). Some of their disadvantages are low memory capacity and low data transfer rate. The cellular phones from the higher class can be used to Internet access via WAP or GPRS technologies. They also can be used to send and receive the multimedia messages (MMS). Their prices continuously decrease.
- *Smart Phones.* They are hybrid devices which combine the abilities of cellular phones and PDA. They have smaller sizes than PDA and bigger than cellular phones. Typically they haven't full sized keyboard and can recognise handwritten text.

M-Learning Access Technology

Mobile access devices are generally used to access electronic learning resources such as e-mail, simple web sites and Virtual Learning Environments (VLEs). Devices may either access these resources ***on-line*** or ***off-line***.

On-line

When on-line, the device is connected directly to learning resources via a network, typically the Internet. This can be achieved in a number of ways including:

- ***Mobile phone connection (GSM, GPRS, UMTS '3G')*** – a mobile phone is used to connect to the internet and either access learning resources via the phone's built in screen or via connecting the phone in turn to a laptop or PDA. GSM, GPRS and UMTS (or '3G') are different mobile phone connection methods.
- ***Wireless LAN connection (WiFi)*** – a laptop or PDA is connected to the Internet through a wireless Local Area Network (LAN). With wireless LANs the network connection between the laptop or PDA and the wall is simply replaced by a radio link. WiFi is emerging as a popular wireless LAN standard and is becoming increasingly available in conference centres, hotels, learning centres and other business venues – even on the beach at Brighton!

Off-line

When off-line, learning resources must first be downloaded from the source e-mail server, web site or VLE to a laptop, PDA or mobile phone then taken out on the move. They can then only be used as standalone resources. The process of downloading (and possibly uploading after modification) learning resources is called ***synchronisation***. Laptops are generally synchronised with learning resources by plugging them directly into a network when back at base. Mobile phones and PDAs are typically synchronised by connecting them to a PC back at base, which is in turn connected to the network. Many phones and PDAs now come with cables and software for doing this.

Data Transmission Modes

Today there are several communication technologies which are used in mobile devices. The following are the some of the data transmission modes:

- Global System for Mobile Communications (GSM): GSM is one of the leading digital cellular systems. It provides integrated voice mail, high-speed data, fax, paging and short message services capabilities, as well as secure communications.

- Wireless Application Protocol (WAP). This is a free, unlicensed protocol for wireless communications. It makes possible creation of advanced communications services and access to Internet pages from a cellular phone.
- General Packet Radio Service (GPRS). A packet-linked technology that enables high-speed wireless Internet and other data communications. GPRS provides about four times greater speed than conventional GSM systems.
- Bluetooth: Bluetooth wireless technology is a short-range radio technology. Bluetooth makes it possible to transmit signals over short distances between telephones, computers and other devices and thereby simplify communication and synchronization between devices.
- IEEE 802.11: It is a type of radio technology used for wireless local area networks (WLANs). It is a standard that has been developed by the IEEE (Institute of Electrical and Electronic Engineers). It is also called wi-fi.
- Infrared Data Association (IrDA). This association defined a suite of protocols for infrared (IR) exchange of data between two devices, up to 1 or 2 meters apart (20 to 30 cm for low-power devices). IrDA devices typically have throughput of up to 115.2Kbps or 4Mbps. Smart phones, many PDAs, printers and laptop computers use IrDA protocols.

Mobile Learning Applications

Mobile learning applications can be sub-divided into six categories:

1. ***Collaborative applications:*** it means that encourage knowledge sharing, making use of the learner's physical location and mobility.
2. ***Location aware applications:*** it means that contextualize information, allowing learners to interact directly with their environment; for example, collecting environmental data linked to geographical context or accessing contextually relevant reference material.
3. ***Data collection applications:*** it means that use the handheld device's ability to record data in the form of text, image, video, and audio.
4. ***Referential applications:*** it means that use dictionaries, translators and e-books to deliver content when and where it is needed.
5. ***Administrative applications:*** it means that employ the typical scheduling, information storage, and other calendar functions available on mobile devices.
6. ***Interactive applications:*** it means that uses both the input and output capabilities of mobile devices, allowing the learner to input information and obtain some form of feedback which aids the learning process.

Key Benefits in Mobile Learning

These are the some of the opportunities to seize mobile learning's unique attributes to improve education:

- ***Promote "anywhere, anytime" learning:*** Mobile devices can be used anywhere, any time, including at offices, home, or when in transit. Mobile devices allow students to gather, access, and process information outside the classroom. They can encourage learning in a real-world context, and help bridge school, after school, and home environments.
- ***Reach economically poor Learner:*** Because of their relatively low cost and accessibility in low-income communities, handheld devices can help advance

digital equity, reaching and inspiring populations "at the edges" children from economically disadvantaged communities and those from developing countries. This technology may contribute to combating the digital divide, as mobile devices are generally cheaper than desktop computers.

- *Develop social interactions:* Its offers an interactive learning experience where learners can interact with each other. Mobile technologies have the power to promote and foster collaboration and communication, which are deemed essential for 21st-century success.
- *Fit with learning environments:* Mobile devices can help overcome many of the challenges associated with larger technologies, as they fit more naturally within various learning environments.
- *Permit a personalized learning experience:* Not all children are alike; instruction should be adaptable to individual and diverse learners. There are significant opportunities for genuinely supporting differentiated, autonomous, and individualized learning through mobile devices.

Key Challenges in Mobile Learning

A number of critical challenges must be addressed to unleash the educational potential of mobile technologies.

- *Negative aspects of mobile learning:* the potential for distraction or unethical behavior; physical health concerns; and data privacy issues.
- *Cultural norms and attitudes:* Though many experts believe that mobile devices have significant potential to transform children's learning, parents and teachers apparently are not yet convinced.
- *No mobile theory of learning:* currently, any widely accepted learning theory for mobile technologies has been established, hampering the effective assessment, pedagogy, and design of new applications for learning.

- ***Differentiated access and technology:*** Wide diversity among mobile technologies represents a challenge for teachers and learners who wish to accelerate academic outcomes as well as the producers who seek to facilitate such learning.
- ***Limiting physical attributes:*** Physical aspects of mobile technologies that may prevent an optimal learning experience include: restricted text entry, small screen size, and limited battery life.
- ***Small Screen:*** The small screens of a mobile or PDA limits the amount and type of information that can displayed at a given time.
- ***Low Storage***: The memory or the storage capacity is limited.
- ***Discharged Battery :*** It is important to have fully functional devices and batteries have to be charged regularly. At times, a discharged battery can result in loss of important data.
- ***Difficult to use:*** It's difficulty to work on moving graphics, especially on mobiles phones, although 3G and 4G will eventually facilitate this.
- ***Low bandwidth:*** Bandwidth may degrade with increasing users when using wireless networks.
- ***Easily lost :*** More easily lost or stolen than desktops, more attractive to thieves than paper notes.
- ***Lack of common platform:*** Lack of common platform (different sized screens – horizontal screens with some handheld computers, small square screens with mobile phones etc.) So difficult to develop content that will work any work.
- ***Out dated***: Fast moving market so devices can become out of date very quickly.

Winding Up

E-learning solutions are needed that are not only on track to address issues of expense and convenience, but also the primary issue of effective learning. Mobile/electronic education should not attempt to replace traditional education with tutors and instructors, but to support both students and teachers by providing services that facilitate teaching, learning and education-related administrative tasks. The basic approach is integrative, combining a variety of devices (mobile and non-mobile) via a variety of transmitting techniques (wired and wireless) which allow migration path to future technologies. The relationships between learners and teachers must be improved and optimized via efficient use of the new technologies. Learning environments must allow learners to personalize their experience to match their own learning styles and expectations. The same goes for the teachers.

Regardless of existing till now disadvantages the m-Learning will became more and more popular with the progress of information and communication technologies. It's common use with the traditional education will correspond to the needs of educational quality improve. The educational process will became more flexible and will fulfil to the needs of life long learning. M-Learning also can assure good educational opportunities for disabled people. So we conclude that m-learning is a next generation of learning.

8.

Blended Learning

Blended Learning: An Introduction

Blended learning (BL) or hybrid learning describes a learning environment that either combines teaching methods, delivery methods, media formats or a mixture of all these. It also refers to the integrated learning activities such as a mixture of online and face-to-face learning. In other words, BL is a mixture of e-learning and traditional types of learning. It is mentioned as the integrated combination of traditional learning with web-based online approaches, the combination of media and tools deployed in an e-learning environment and the combination of a number of pedagogical approaches. Among the benefits of BL reported by recent researches were (i) provide students with more control over learning; (ii) help foster critical thinking; (iii) effectiveness of online assessment system and computer tutorials.

Objectives of Blended Learning Program

There are varieties of objective for implementing a blended learning program, as follows:

1. Improved learning effectiveness, over either pure traditional classroom learning or pure e-learning.
2. Increased convenience (time, place and so on).
3. Cost savings: The cost savings may result from perhaps reducing the number of instructors.
4. Classroom space savings for the school: The e-learning component of a blended learning program can help ease the classroom space needs by having students learn more from outside the classrooms. The freed-

up classroom space can potentially be used for other purposes.

5. Reduced traffic and parking jamming on the campus.

Elements in Blended Learning

Blended learning includes a combination of computer-based and/or on-line and face-to-face elements, and a mix of formats, media, and methods, so the most appropriate and effective approach can be used for each part of the learning experience.

Formats

- You may work face-to-face with students or they may work independently in a self-paced way.
- Your conference place could be something like a classroom, community centre room, conference hall, computer lab, etc.
- You and/or your students may work some of the time in a computer lab.
- You may suggest learners join on-line learning communities and discussions.
- You may suggest learners attempt Web-based tutorials or activities.

Media

- You may utilize CDs, videotapes, audio tapes, books, newspapers, television, radio, on-line chat, computers, Web sites, and games.
- Some of these media (for example, newspapers or games) are available or usable on-line or as a physical resource.

Methods

- You may work one-on-one with students.
- You may set up group projects.
- You may put different groups together to work on similar topics or projects.

Dimensions of the Blend

The original use of the phrase "Blended Learning" was often associated with simply linking traditional classroom training to eLearning activities. However, the term has evolved to encompass a much richer set of learning strategy "dimensions." Today a blended learning programme may combine one or more of the following dimensions, although many of these have over-lapping attributes.

Blending Offline and Online Learning

At the simplest level, a blended leaning experience combines offline and online forms of learning where the online learning usually means "over the Internet or intranet," and offline learning happens in a more traditional classroom setting. We assume that even the offline learning offerings are managed through an online learning system. An example of this type of blending may include a learning program that provides study materials and research resources over the Web while providing instructor-led, classroom training sessions as the main medium of instruction.

Blending Self-Paced and Live, Collaborative Learning

Self-paced learning implies solitary, on-demand learning at a pace that is managed or controlled by the learner. Collaborative learning on the other hand implies a more dynamic communication among many learners that brings about knowledge sharing. The blending of self-paced and collaborative learning may include review of important literature on a regulatory change or new product followed by a moderated, live online, peer-to-peer discussion of the material's application to the learner's job and customers.

Blending Structured and Unstructured Learning

Not all forms of learning imply a pre-meditated, structured or formal learning program with organized content in specific sequence like chapters in a text book. In fact, most learning in the workplace occurs in an unstructured form such as meetings, hallway conversations, and e-mail. A blended program design may look to capture active conversations and documents from unstructured learning events into knowledge repositories available on-demand, supporting the way knowledge-workers collaborate and work.

Blending Custom Content with Off-the-Shelf Content

Off-the-shelf content is by definition generic - unaware of your organization's unique context and requirements. However, generic content is much less expensive to buy and frequently has higher production values than custom content you build yourself. Generic, self-paced content can be customized today with a blend of live experiences (classroom or online) or through content customization. Industry standards such as SCORM (Shareable Courseware Object Reference Model) open the door to greater flexibility in blending off-the-shelf and custom content - improving the user experience while minimizing cost.

Blending Work and Learning

Ultimately, the true success and effectiveness of learning in organizations is believed to be associated with the paradigm where work (such as business applications) and learning are inseparable, and where learning is embedded in business processes such as hiring, sales, or product development. Work becomes a source of learning content to be shared and more learning content becomes accessible on-demand and in the context of the user's workplace need.

Categories of Blended Learning Systems

There are three categories of blended learning program, as follows:

Enabling blends: Primarily focus on addressing issues of access and convenience—for example, blends that are intended to provide additional flexibility to the learners or blends that attempt to provide the same opportunities or learning experience but through a different modality.

Enhancing blends: Allow incremental changes to the pedagogy but do not radically change the way teaching and learning occurs. This can occur at both ends of the spectrum. For example, in a traditional face-to-face learning environment, additional resources and perhaps some supplementary materials may be included online.

Transforming blends: Blends that allow a essential transformation of the pedagogy—for example, a change from a model where learners are just receivers of information to a model where learners actively construct knowledge through dynamic interactions. These types of blends enable intellectual activity that was not practically possible without the technology.

Benefits of Blended Learning

There are many benefits to blended learning. The list contains the following items:

- Students can participate at any time.
- Students can collaborate on their own time.
- It can provide reduction in costs, time, labour, stress, etc.
- Course documents are available to learner 24 hours a day.
- Flexible classroom scheduling.
- Class goals can easily be met.
- Uniformed classes for multi-section offerings.
- Effective use of class time
- Enhanced computer literacy among students and instructors.
- Using the World Wide Web resources to support class activities.
- Supply students with additional learning materials if they need them.

- Increase the quality of communications between the instructor and learner.
- Using interactive programs that produce quick feedback and an advice for any remedial work.

Difficulties to Blended Learning

Despite the advantages, there are some difficulties with blended learning. These can be reduced or overcome. To avoid these points might reduce the quality of teaching in this mode. These might include:

Bias: Some people have difficulty using or accepting teaching methods that are unfamiliar or unconventional. In the case of computer mediated learning, some people cannot use computers well or prefer to avoid using them. Blended learning can be adapted to suit not only the learners but also the teachers.

Faculty difficulties: Faculty compensation and initial difficulties to cope up with the learning requirement to teach in this mode. Not all instructors are as effective in teaching blended courses.

Lack of means: One may not have enough time, money, equipment, etc. E-learning classes cannot function if instructors and students cannot operate the necessary hardware and software. Some schools may not have enough computer rooms for every teacher to use one, a school may not even have computers at all, or a teacher may not have the time or skills to create computer activities for lessons. Lack of time to train on various technological tools.

Poor mixes: Learning methods and tools need to be used well in conjunction with each other. Careful thought needs to go into making a good blend.

Computer difficulties: Students might have different computers with different bandwidth capabilities. Different speed of computers used by the students.

Conclusion

A common feature in blended lessons is that students work in pairs or groups to complete a task. Education is not just information transfer but also skill development and social interaction. Students learn from each other as they help one another through the tasks and observe each others, work. Blended learning can provide reduction in costs, time, labour, stress, etc. Normally this is achieved by using computers. Materials kept on line are easier to access, distribute, and reproduce. Material can be accessed instantly from many locations at any time. This saves not only time, it also saves money that would be used for printing and distributing, and natural resources that would become paper waste. In addition it saves learners from losing, forgetting, or having to carry texts. Teachers can more easily share work with other teachers, and teachers can more easily modify and upgrade material. A blended learning approach can make teaching easier.

9.

U-Learning

Introduction: U-Learning

Education has undergone major changes in recent years, with the development of digital information transfer, storage and communication methods having a significant effect. This development has allowed for access to global communications and the number of resources available to today's students at all levels of schooling. Now, the assimilation of ubiquitous computing in education marks another great step forward, with Ubiquitous Learning (u-learning) emerging through the concept of ubiquitous computing.

After the initial impact and applications of computers in education, the introduction of e-learning and mobile learning epitomized the constant transformations that were occurring in education.

What does u-learning mean?

U-learning means "everywhere learning" (the internet or learning content follows people around). Core "knowledge pots" (work-related content, personal knowledge, internet) hold content and information. Various devices plug in and retrieve the information in the appropriate format (PDA, cell phone, laptop, or any other technology gadgets). It fulfills e-learning's promise of "anytime, anywhere, and any context".

A ubiquitous learning environment is any setting in which students can become totally immersed in the learning process. To define:

Ubiquitous = pervasive, omnipresent, ever present, everywhere

Learning = educational, instructive, didactic, pedagogical

Environment = surroundings, setting, situation, atmosphere

So, a ubiquitous learning environment (ULE) is a situation or setting of pervasive (or omnipresent) education (or learning). Education is happening all around the student but the student may not even be conscious of the learning process.

Concept of U-Learning

Mark Weiser coined the term 'Ubiquitous Computing (UC)' in the late 1980s. He introduced the idea of ubiquitous computing: a world in which computers and associated technologies become invisible, and thus indistinguishable from everyday life. He also further indicated that Ubiquitous Computing is the method of enhancing computer use by making many computers available throughout the physical environment, but making them effectively invisible to the user. Based on the Weiser's view, UC refers to the process of seamlessly integrating computers into the physical world, in which the presence of computers is becoming less conspicuous and will eventually blend into our daily lives.

A ubiquitous computing technology-equipped system supplies users with timely information and relevant services by automatically sensing users' various context data and smartly generating proper results. So the characteristics of a pervasive computing environment can be mainly concluded as the following: User mobility, Resource and location discovery, Context awareness (user/time/location), Collaborative interaction, Ambient information, Calm technology, Event notification, Adaptive interfaces, Invisibility object augmentation, and Anytime/anywhere.

Essentially, U-learning is the extend and advance of E-learning, and also can be viewed as a combination of the advantages of E-learning and M-learning with the benefits of ubiquitous computing and the flexibility of mobile devices. Students have the freedom to learn within a learning environment, which offers adaptability to their individual needs and learning styles, as well as the flexibility of pervasive and unobtrusive computer systems.

Components of u-learning

U-learning made from two components. That is e-learning and m-learning. The term e-learning covers a wide set of applications and processes, including computer-based learning, web-based learning, virtual classrooms and digital collaboration. We define e-learning as the delivery of content via all electronic media, including the Internet, Intranets, Extranets, satellite broadcast, audio/video tape, interactive TV, and CD-ROM. Yet, e-learning is defined more narrowly than distance learning, which would include text-based learning and courses conducted via written correspondence.

M-learning is a subset of e-learning. E-learning is the macro concept that includes online and mobile learning environments. In this regard the following simple definition of Quin (2001) is very useful: 'M-learning is e-learning through mobile computational devices: Palms, windows CE machines, even your digital cell phone.'

Characteristics of Ubiquitous Learning

The following are the important characteristics of ubiquitous learning:

1. *Permanency:* Learners never lose their work unless it is purposefully deleted. In addition, all the learning processes are recorded continuously everyday.

2. *Accessibility:* Learners have access to their documents, data, or videos from anywhere. That information is provided based on their requests. Therefore, the learning involved is self-directed.

3. *Immediacy:* Wherever learners are, they can get any information immediately. Thus, learners can solve problems quickly. Otherwise, the learner can record the questions and look for the answer later.

4. *Interactivity:* Learners can interact with experts, teachers, or peers in the form of synchronies or asynchronous communication. Hence, the experts are more reachable and the knowledge becomes more available.

5. *Situating of instructional activities:* The learning could be embedded in our daily life. The problems encountered as well as the knowledge required are all presented in their natural and authentic forms. This helps learners notice the features of problem situations that make particular actions relevant.

6. *Adaptability:* Learners can get the right information at the right place with the right way.

Types of U-Learning

These are a few of the most common types of U-learning.

(a) *Mobile Based Learning (MBL)* : mobile devices accompany users in their everyday experiences and become a convenient source of information or means of communication that assists with learning. Mobile devices provide just-in-time access to learning resources, news information, planners, address books, calculators, and so forth.

(b) *Technology-Based Learning (TBL)* : Technology-based learning includes deployment of methods that use recent technological developments such as computer-mediated communication, videoconferencing, multi-media, groupware, video on demand, desktop publishing, intelligent tutoring system, virtual reality and so on.

(c) *Web-Based Training (WBT)* : Generally web-based learning, e-learning uses streaming media, text, and graphics to develop exciting learning environment that is deployed right on the user via the internet. In that method, Learning takes place through Internet.

(d) ***Synchronous e-learning :*** Synchronous e-learning means learning and teaching takes place at the same time while the trainer and learners are physically separated from each other. Synchronous leanings are as follows: Internet telephony, Web conferencing, Online lectures, and Audio/video conferencing.

(e) ***Asynchronous e-learning :*** Asynchronous e-learning means that the user can take the training indent of any schedule. Asynchronous e-learning does not need a facilitator or instructor. Asynchronous e-learning are the following: Self-paced courses taken via internet on CD-ROM, Stored audio/video level presentations or seminars.

Benefits of U-Learning

The following are the some of the benefits of ubiquitous learning.

Any where and any time : A participant can access the learning programme at any time that is convenient -not just during the specific 1-3-hour period that is set for a conventional course. The participants do not have to meet. That means they can be anywhere. International sharing is feasible. Individuals can log on at work, home, the library, in a community-learning center or from their hotel when traveling.

Faster learning : With U-learning students will learn up to twice as much in half the time that they would in classroom teaching. This is because the course progresses as fast as the students can without worry for other student or an instruction.

Consistent instruction : Every instructor has his or her own style, which may not be best for students learning. Some days the instructor is in top form and delivers a great class. Other days he or she may be bored, tired or simply unmotivated. With u-learning the course is software driven and each student receives the same high quality content.

No need for a classroom : In u-learning there are no actual classrooms, no teachers or textbooks, but it gives the impression of studying in a classroom

Reduced overall cost : Reduced overall cost is the single most influential factor in adopting u-learning. The elimination of costs associated with instructor's salaries, meeting room rentals, and student travel, lodging, and meals are directly quantifiable.

Available at 24/7/365 : With U-learning students will learn at any time. ie 24 hours per day/ 7 days per week / 365 days per year. Learners can work late into the night, in short sessions distributed throughout the day, or in long blocks of time; whatever works best for them.

Group collaboration : Electronic messaging creates new opportunities for groups to work together; creating shared electronic conversations that can be thoughtful and more permanent than voice conversations. Sometimes aided by on-line moderators, these net seminars can be powerful for learning and problem solving. Now a day the students can communicate with their friends and teachers through mobile.

Suggestions to Make U-Learning Possible In India

The following are some of the suggestions to make u-learning possible in India:

- UGC should give the sponsor to the college, those who are organizing the seminar or conference related to e-learning and m-learning.
- Try to make the wifi facilities to all the colleges.
- Minimize the cost of computers and motivate the learners to purchase computers by offering loans with minimum interest/ interest free loan.
- Tax free for computers and mobiles.
- As Internet functioning needs the use of telephone, telephony should be technologically improved and the

government should make all the local calls free, thereby Internet accessing will become cheaper.

- Internet facilities should be provided to the rural areas and computer literacy program needs to be conducted in rural areas.
- UGC, ASC, NCERT and NCTE should give the orientation programme to the lectures related to u-learning environment.
- Make the knowledge of computer compulsory for all types of recruitments.
- Develop the habit of reading through computer monitors and mobile screens.

Conclusion

Now it is an information era. The students are willing to learn the new technologies like mobile phones, i-pod, i-phone, internet etc. This allows more creative and independent learning. To maintain standard or quality in education, one should make use of electronic technology in teaching learning process. The recent technology of our world is ubiquitous technology. U-learning is developing in higher speed. Surly we will accept that the next generation of learning is u-learning.

Index

F

G